Vodka Soup for the Widowed Soul

Vodka Soup for the Widowed Soul

Stories of Grief, Alcohol, Infidelity, Cursing, and Hope

Michelle Miller

© 2018 Michelle Miller
Cover art by Paul Ribera
All rights reserved.
ISBN: 1981880437
ISBN-13: 9781981880430
Library of Congress Control Number: 2017919566
CreateSpace Independent Publishing Platform
North Charleston, South Carolina

This book is dedicated to those who grieve and do so without eloquence or pretension. This book is also dedicated to Eminem, Slim Shady, and Marshall Mathers

Table of Contents

Part 1	Why I Lost My Shit	1
Chapter 1	The Masturbating Woman	3
Chapter 2	From MyDiary	7
Chapter 3	This Isn't Me	9
Chapter 4	The Night My Husband Shot Himself	11
Chapter 5	My Widow Brain Wrote This Book	13
Part 2	Losing My Shit	17
Chapter 6	Happy Anniversary to Me!	19
Chapter 7	Things I Wrote on My Facebook Wall on My Husband's Birthday	23
Chapter 8	Dinosaurs	27
Chapter 9	I Pretend I Am Bold Like Lynnette	31
Chapter 10	The Bomb Shelter	33
Chapter 11	From John's Blog: Goodbye	41
Chapter 12	How to Drop the Widow Bomb on Your Date in Three Easy Steps	43
Chapter 13	The Tiny Fragments	47
Chapter 14	Not a Widow	53
Chapter 15	What I Told My Children about Their Father's Suicide	59

Chapter 16	September Rain	65
Chapter 17	A Hammer	67
Chapter 18	From John's Blog: Battling Demons	69
Chapter 19	The Anger Orgasm	71
Chapter 20	No	77
Chapter 21	Depression Takes	79
Chapter 22	From John's Blog: Thoughts of Pain	83
Chapter 23	Widow-Phobia	85
Chapter 24	Grief in the Shower	89
Chapter 25	The Formal Air	91
Chapter 26	My Chapter Two Does Not Have a Penis	93
Chapter 27	Dust	97
Chapter 28	Fourteen New Year's Resolutions for the Widowed	101
Chapter 29	Choices and Cheeseburgers: How We Spent the One-Year Anniversary of His Suicide	103
Chapter 30	My Diary Entries from the Affair Years	109
Chapter 31	Why Don't You and Jesus Pick Up the Dog Shit?	113
Chapter 32	Hairapist versus a Therapist	117
Chapter 33	Lived	119
Chapter 34	Four Widow-Approved Ways to Avoid the Holi-daze	121
Chapter 35	The Nerve	127
Chapter 36	Things I Wrote on my Facebook for Our Wedding Anniversary	129
Chapter 37	From John's Blog: Feeling Word of the Day	133
Chapter 38	Thirteen Ways That Widows Are like Toddlers	135
Chapter 39	Zombie	141
Chapter 40	The Tears of His Mother	145
Chapter 41	Teal with Bright Yellow Stars	147
Chapter 42	Five Shitty Things People Said to Me after His Suicide	149
Chapter 43	The F-Word	151
Chapter 44	I Wore a White Dress to My Husband's Funeral	155
Chapter 45	Was My Husband's Suicide a Choice?	157
Chapter 46	Why I Stayed	161
Chapter 47	From John's Blog: Sleepless Morning Rant	165

Chapter 48	Rage Widow and Her French Fries	167
Chapter 49	Band-Aids	171
Chapter 50	Stand	173
Chapter 51	My Husband's Last Day on Earth	179
Chapter 52	Bathit Crazy Joy	185
Chapter 53	From John's Blog: Meds and Feeling Check	191
Chapter 54	The Sex Buffet	193
Chapter 55	Sit	197
Chapter 56	My Diary: What If?	199
Chapter 57	Wonder Widow	201
Chapter 58	Strip Darts	205
Chapter 59	A Nice Man	209
Chapter 60	The Brown Leather Jacket	211
Chapter 61	I'd Rather Be Phillip's Wife Than John's Widow	215
Chapter 62	Things I Wrote on Facebook on His Death Anniversary	219
Chapter 63	Cremation Jewelry	223
Chapter 64	From John's Blog: Forest Gump	227
Chapter 65	Three Things to Say to a Widow	229
Chapter 66	I Miss	233
Chapter 67	Cocktail Recipes for Life after Your Husband's Affair	235
Chapter 68	They'll Wind Up at Harvard One Day	237
Chapter 69	I Just Knew	239
Chapter 70	Mashed Potatoes	245
Chapter 71	Hope	251
Chapter 72	When I Started to Slowly Stop Hating God	253
Chapter 73	Candy, Wine Bottles, Erections	255
Chapter 74	Hair Dye	261
Chapter 75	From John's Final Blog: One Good Day	269
Part 3	Gathering Up My Shit	271
Chapter 76	Sleeping Again after You Pee	273

Can't Get Enough of Me? · · · · · · · · · · · 279

Part 1

Why I Lost My Shit

"Hence, the stroke."

-M‍YSELF

Chapter 1

The Masturbating Woman

September 2011

I instantly recognized the masturbating woman in his saved e-mail file. I could hear her children playing in the next room. I could see her wedding photos on the wall behind the bed she was lying (and sometimes bent over) on. I admired her cherry bed frame as she began moaning my husband's name.

My husband's name.

"Joooooohn. Joooooooooooooooohn."

This was my husband's first death. His final death would be by suicide two and a half years after the masturbating woman made her debut on our family computer.

My tongue swelled and itched. My fingers started tingling, cramped into fists, and then curled into my forearms involuntarily. The left side of my body went numb, and then I blacked out. WebMD and I later diagnosed myself with a stress-induced stroke.

I was unconscious for a little over five minutes, according to my microwave clock. During those five minutes, I could still hear the masturbation videos above the ringing in my ears, but I was physically paralyzed by the realization that my marriage vows had been severed. What I knew for sure, in my unconscious state, is that two bodies really do become one when you cleave to your spouse, and I also knew that John had removed his body from my body.

Hence, the stroke.

When my vision returned, I looked up at the computer screen from a puddle of sweat on the kitchen tile. I watched the rest of the masturbation videos while I regained feeling in my extremities. A sudden surge of adrenaline catapulted me off the floor and to the kitchen sink, where I vomited until I passed out again. My garbage disposal was never the same after this, and neither was I.

I was only unconscious for less than a minute the second time around. I willed myself awake and crawled back over to the computer to rewatch the collection of videos. And then I watched them again. And again. I watched the entire collection of masturbation videos three times in a row.

The pain I inflicted on myself that day as I chose to watch and rewatch the videos, and the pain I would be inflicting on myself in the years to come by demanding to know every single detail of my husband's long history of adultery, was a testament to how very much I hated myself.

Women who love themselves simply do not watch their husband's married girlfriend masturbate three times in a row.

Rewatching these videos was also a testament to how desperate I was to regain the control I'd thought I had during my marriage. If I memorized his secrets, they were no longer *his* secrets. They were *our* reality. It's funny to me now that I wanted this woman's waxed vulva to be a part of our reality.

Rewatching these videos was also a testament to how much I needed validation. My husband had been telling me for months that I was crazy. He'd been telling me for months that my female intuition was deceiving me. With each stroke of her fingers, I was validated. However, this validation came at a high price. You can't unsee the things you see, and you can't unknow what you now know to be true.

Still, I do not regret watching them. What I do regret is that when I confronted my husband that night, John didn't tell me everything he'd been hiding. The slow trickle of the truth over the next two and a half years was like being tortured within an inch of my life every day, only to be revived and tortured again using an entirely new and increasingly cruel technique. Yes, I wish he would've told me everything that first night.

Everything.

It would've killed me instantly, and I would have preferred death to the things I had to endure after this day.

Chapter 2

From MyDiary

December 28, 2013-eighty-six days before his suicide
I fucking hate that worthless, fucking asshole son-of-a-bitch bastard, and I hope he dies.

Chapter 3

This Isn't Me

This is a portion of John's suicide note. I chose not to have the spelling and grammar edited as I feel it would have lessened the impact of his voice. The same goes for the excerpts of his blog that have been scattered throughout this book.

March 23, 2014

I am in so much pain right now and nothing will help it but this. My mind and my heart has been dead for a while now but my body hasn't caught on so i am helping it realize. I can't eat. I can't sleep. I can't make it through a day without crying. No amount of pills or booze in this world will make this even remotely tolerable. Because all those things still aren't you and the kids, my life, my purpose. Please try to make it through this text and be as strong as I know you are.

I have been thinking a lot lately about how nothing lasts forever like I thought it would. I thought our marriage will last forever. I thought our love would last forever. And with this divorce that has changed the way I feel about all that. I am scared that my love for you will eventually fade away. So that is why I am doing this now. I still love you more than ever and that is a feeling that I cannot loose. Life doesn't last forever but at least my love for you will last forever this way.

Everything that I have been working on for the last 10 years now has no purpose and is gone. My kids are gone. My wife is gone. My dogs are gone. My life is gone. There is no purpose in me being here anymore. Please try to remember the good traits about me and try to pass them on to the kids.

Try not to remember me in this state. This isn't me.

This is the shell that is left after everything was lost. Read my blog and remember who I was. I love you all so much and am very blessed to have the time I had with everyone that I have met throughout the years. The good years and the bad ones.

My car will be up at the quarry area at the top of ft Irwin rd right before the bend. The place where we ate del taco together once and watched the sunset. It will be locked and the key will be under the front driver side tire. My body will be a little ways away towards barstow so that you don't have to see the spot where I died. Just call 911 and have them send someone up to pick up the body. Sorry again for all this but I didn't want to commit suicide in the house. I want you and the kids to enjoy the house like you used to.

It is a very lonely place without the sound of the kids laughter.

I love you more than you could ever imagine Michelle. So proud that you let me give you my last name. I love you. Forever.

The next day I decided to go back to my maiden name Michelle Miller, because suicide is not fucking romantic.

Chapter 4

The Night My Husband Shot Himself

March 23, 2014

The gun was in his car when he pulled up to my parents' house to give me my mail and say good night to the kids. In the two months since we'd separated, he'd never done this. I should have known.

Fifteen minutes later, I got his suicide note through text messaging. I didn't read the entirety of it until the day after his death, and then I read it every day for months and months.

Three sentences into the first lengthy paragraph, I called John, while my dad called the police and his parents. He answered the phone immediately and told me that he was just outside of town, alone with a shotgun, somewhere in the Mojave Desert.

My dad and I drove out to where we thought he might be, on a northbound single-lane highway, until the police stopped us. And that is where we spent the next two hours: on the side of the highway, sun descending on the cloudless horizon, dusty breeze picking up speed as the minutes wore on, and my cell phone in my hand as I begged him to drop the gun.

I only remember a handful of sentences John and I spoke to each other during those two hours. There was a point when I realized he had turned. I am not being melodramatic when I say that his voice became demonic sounding. I had been watching John, the real John, slip from me for years now, and the change in his voice just as the sun set behind the barren, desert hills told me he was gone for good.

I want to say something romantic here, something about how I finally let go of my husband that day with the setting of the sun. I want to say something about how I finally accepted that the man I had married eight years ago had been dead for a while, that maybe he never really existed in the first place. I want to say something about how I knew our deep-rooted love would sustain me even after he was gone. But the truth of that moment was the very opposite of romance: I felt relieved that he was about to die.

I was relieved that I would not have to endure a divorce from a controlling, abusive sex addict. I was relieved that my kids would not have to be shuttled back and forth between a stable house and a house full of women and oppression. I was relieved that all the secrets I had been keeping for years about my marriage were about to be exposed and that my mental and physical decline since 2011 would be understood and validated. One day, I would find it in me to be relieved for John, too.

When his voice turned demonic, I stopped trying to talk the shotgun out of his hands, and I just listened to him weep inconsolably while I took deep breaths, bracing myself for the inevitable. When his last words, "I can't…Good-bye. I love you," were spoken to me, he carried out the act with his phone still on. He wanted me to hear everything.

I never heard the gunshot, though. All I heard were his screams.

Chapter 5

My Widow Brain Wrote This Book

2017

This book is an extension of my erratic, confused, and (possibly) inebriated widow brain. The stories, blogs, advice, lists, and rants in Part Two of this book are in no particular order. I tried my damnedest to make them flow into some sort of cohesive story, but alas, like most of my widowhood "relationshits," at the two-month mark, I stopped trying to make sense of things and just let them be what they were meant to be: chaos.

Feel free to read the next part in this book in order, or skip around… or do what I would do, which is skip to the chapters with titles that sound like they might have something to do with sex. Read only those chapters, and then put this book on your bookshelf, and dust it once every year. Just kidding—widows don't dust.

Also, names of the guilty have been changed and all that jazz. The stories that involve my children have been shared with their permission. Don't sue me; I am an impoverished writer, and if you think a character in this book is you and that you have been poorly represented, just tell yourself that it wasn't you.

Oh, and one last thing before you dive into the madness: I was too lazy to elaborate on certain people in this book, so flip back to this chapter if you need a more detailed description of a specific person.

*Allyssa: Friend whom I admire (also see "am insanely jealous of"). She was widowed seven months before me.
*Amber: My most favorite person to karaoke with.
*Chad, Tim, James, Ky, Jeremy, Matthew, and Lenny: Random guys I had grief sex with. No, those aren't their real names, because I don't remember their real names.
*Crays/Cray: Crazy, fun, interesting people who get it.
*Garrett: My son and my youngest child. Age seven at the time of his dad's death.
*Guilt Bunny: The pet bunny you buy for your kids after their dad dies that you have convinced yourself will make everything better.
*Ho1: The first of my husband's girlfriends, the one I found masturbating in his saved e-mail file that caused my stress-induced stroke. She's fifteen years older than me, married (still), and has some kids.
*Ho2: The second of my husband's girlfriends. Younger than me. Married, has a few kids…none of whom were fathered by her husband, I think.
*Ho3: The third of my husband's girlfriends but the first one he started cheating with in the early days of our relationship, as far as I know. Single. Oh, and according to pictures, her breasts are grossly lopsided.
*Hot Neighbor: A neighbor who is hot.
*Isabelle/Belle: My daughter and my eldest. Age eleven at the time of her dad's death.
*John: My late husband. We wed in 2005, and he died in 2014, at the age of twenty-nine.
*Kate: My long-distance best friend.
*Lauri: My Camp Widow best friend. (Camp Widow is a thing! Check out CampWidow.org.)

*Lynnette: My best friend of seventeen years. Also my current roommate and nonsexual life partner.
*Norms/Norm: Normal, nontraumatized people.
*Phillip: A guy that I loved.
*Veronica: "Friend" seems too trite. Let's call her a family member.

Part 2

Losing My Shit

"Don't go in the portable toilet on your right; go to the one on your left. You cannot unsee the things you will see in the portable toilet on your right."

–MYSELF

Chapter 6

Happy Anniversary to Me!

What no one tells you about trauma is that it can make you very horny. I was pondering this strange reaction to John's affair as we drove up to a cabin in the mountains for our six-year wedding anniversary shortly after Ho1's masturbation videos premiered in my kitchen. I was rabid with desire for him. He, in turn, not only refused to have sex with me since the affair revelation, but he also physically recoiled at even the most casual of my touches.

Happy anniversary to me!

As we ascended the mountain that day, I didn't realize that I had been traumatized; denial forced me to downplay my kitchen-floor vomit experience from "traumatic" to "dramatic." Yes, denial told me I was just being overly dramatic about a very common problem that most marriages faced.

What no one tells you about this very common problem is that it is not like the movies. At least, my affair experience wasn't. There had been no tearful confession or apology from John when I confronted him. There had been no sympathy for my shattered heart. In the absence of these things, there was blame directed toward me and the threat that if I told anyone, I would find myself going through a divorce.

The only logical step after this conversation was obviously for me to plan a romantic anniversary getaway to the mountains. So I did.

I had packed a string bikini for the hot tub and a bottle of Bacardi for the pain. If I could give you only one piece of advice for trauma aftermath, it would be to start drinking. Yes, start drinking, and then one day you will realize that the fun, out-of-control feeling that comes with binge drinking is a metaphor for how completely out of control grief makes you feel. Alcohol will also make you realize you never really had control to begin with. You will also realize one day that using alcohol (and anything else) to dull pain is enjoyable but futile, because eventually you will have to just learn to exist within the pain or die trying to medicate it.

Most of us can't reach this enlightenment until we hit rock bottom. The sooner you start binge drinking on your wedding anniversary, the closer you are to rock bottom, so drink up!

It had been six years since I'd worn a string bikini and three years since I'd had alcohol, and I figured this would be a good time to bring them both back into my life because I had become boring. Yes, John's tiny indiscretion had happened because I had become boring with my hot, home-cooked meals at 6:30 p.m. every night. I'd become stale as I raised our two children, worked, kept a clean house, and had sex with him four times a week.

Yes. Four times a week.

Yawn.

If you get nothing else from this book, I need you to understand that not only did I enjoy having frequent sex with my husband, but I was also good at it, too. Now I basically lay there, facedown in the couch cushion of some bachelor pad, praying to Beyoncé that the nameless guy behind me won't see me crying about my dead husband.

I had decided in my state of denial that our anniversary weekend would be the beginning of me being exciting again. I would be free-spirited and sexy, like I was when we had first met, seven and a half years ago. I would open his beer cans. I would take shots of Bacardi with him. I would laugh at his jokes. I would stroke his ego. I would wear false eyelashes and style my hair. I would be *her*.

I wonder how many times she woke up on the pink bathroom floor of a cabin in her own vomit, I thought the next morning as I mopped the contents of my stomach up with the fresh white guest towels.

So much for me being sexy and exciting.

Although, I had managed to free the spirits in my stomach from the night before, so maybe I was on the right track.

John was still asleep in the middle of the king-sized bed as I started the shower. The hot water ran down my frail, shaking body, and foggy memories of the night started to come into focus. I remembered his indifference as I revealed to him my hot-pink string bikini. I remember opening that fifth beer for him and wondering if he was drunk enough to finally give in to having sex with me. I remember that we did have sex. I remember my vagina tingling as we had the sex because I couldn't stop thinking about how his penis had recently been inside of *her*. I remember him commenting on how thin I had become and then telling me to get off of him. And then I remembered what brought me into the bathroom to throw up in the first place: he'd confessed to me that he had been hiding a decade-long sex and pornography addiction.

Again, happy anniversary to me!

We'd drain our savings account over the next two years on marriage counseling, individual counseling, self-help books, and outpatient sex-addiction recovery programs. John would only get worse. He'd sleep less, eat strange foods, and his moods would become increasingly unpredictable. When our marriage counselor told him to see a psychiatrist because he had symptoms of bipolar disorder and depression, John would refuse. Over the next two and a half years, this man—whose chin stubble I can still feel on my face when I close my eyes—became unrecognizable to me.

But this book is not about him and his decline. It is about me and mine.

When I got out of the shower that morning, I knew just what to do to save our marriage: I was going to be nice. I began writing a list of one hundred things that I loved about him while wrapped in a towel in that mauve bathroom. I would present it to him that night at dinner. Yes, I was going to love John back to me. I was going to love him enough for the both of us.

I was going to shut my mouth.

I was going to listen to his commands.

I was going to be prettier.

I was going to buy him presents.

I was going to encourage him to spend unlimited amounts of time with his friends, even though they had aided in his affair.

I was going to be his own personal porn girl and smother him with daily nude pictures of myself.

I was going to perform sex acts that made me uncomfortable.

I was going to get up at 5:00 a.m. and cook him breakfast in addition to his nightly dinners.

I was going to turn the other cheek when he insulted me.

I was going to be Jesus (except for the porn girl part, because I really do believe Jesus was celibate and not a girl).

The thing about Jesus, though, was that no matter how nice he was, no matter how much love he showed to everyone, no matter how much he sacrificed for the good of others, at the end of it all, he was still flogged and crucified by the very same people he saved.

Chapter 7

Things I Wrote on My Facebook Wall on My Husband's Birthday

September 22, 2017

He was born thirty-three years ago today with a brain predisposed to illness. I'm amazed now to think that he made it through twenty-nine years here on this merciless planet before pulling that trigger. How frightening this world must've been for him, the boy born with the ticking time bomb in his head.

I've never felt that I had the right to mourn him on the anniversary of the day he was born. It seems that this day should belong to his family, the ones who knew the "real" him—the innocent little boy. The one who was happy after simply running through the desert, the one who never even considered that one day he would die by his own hand in that very same desert.

I never knew him, but I did love him. I don't think I'll ever fully reconcile this contrast. Today I will grieve for the little boy I never knew, not the man who turned out to be a stranger to me.

September 22, 2016

Dear John,

Time does not heal. Time makes your absence more absolute. Time makes the weathered threads from your Dickies jacket that lives under my bed unravel at my touch. Time takes away the vividness of the good memories and magnifies the bad.

What did you smell like? Was it Swisher Sweets with a hint of engine grease and a dash of Head & Shoulders shampoo, or was the engine grease more prominent? How did your voice sound in the middle of the night when neither of us could sleep?

I don't remember.

I remember your callousness when I caught you cheating. I remember your indifference when the therapist told you to see a psychiatrist. I remember your temper.

Which one were you—the hard worker fragranced with engine grease, whose voice lulled me to sleep, or the apathetic adulterer who blamed me for your inability to drop the gun?

Because today is your birthday, I'm obligated by society to recall only the good things about you. Fuck obligation. Today I will lament over both sides of you: the forgotten and the remembered, the good and the bad.

This is progress from your last two postmortem birthdays, when I forced myself to focus so precisely on your bad sides that I spent the months after them convinced you had no good sides.

You had good sides.

Today I will not dehumanize you by recalling only the good; you hated it when people did this to the deceased. Today I will not dehumanize you by recalling only the bad; I don't have the kind of energy required to maintain this lie.

The truth is you were everything. You were all the things that exist between good and bad and birth and death, and I will be thinking of all of these things as the kids and I eat your birthday cake today.

September 22, 2015
Happy thirty-first birthday to my late husband, John. A man who was chronically and incurably lonely. A man who never realized

that all the things he craved here on earth—the serenity of being understood, the wholeness of unconditional love, the relief of forgiveness, and the satisfaction of being appreciated—had been given to him all along. A man who never accepted how deeply loved he was by so many people. A man who never saw himself through the eyes of my children who still wear his T-shirts to bed each night.

September 22, 2014
I've been trying to find the "right" picture, song, or words since 4:00 a.m. There aren't any.
Happy thirtieth birthday, John.

Chapter 8

Dinosaurs

I should have never had children.

On the one-hour drive to my in-laws' house, I can't keep this mantra from repeating in my head as I become hypnotized by the sound of the tires on the pavement.

I should have never had children.

The fight the kids are having in the back seat over the iPad brings me out of my trance, and I snap at them, telling them to behave, *or else*…as if I would actually have the energy to do anything.

My children are a burden. Because of them, I still have to be around John's family, the family I was supposed to be permanently detached from when John and I got divorced. Now, I'm stuck with people who blame me for his death and hate me. No, they've never said it, but why wouldn't they feel that way? It's the truth. If it weren't for me, their only son/brother/nephew/cousin/grandson would still be alive. The guilt is physically painful when I am around them. It's in my bones, my muscles, my stomach, and my head; sometimes I can feel the guilt in the strands of my hair. I realize that makes no sense, but you're just going to have to trust me on that one. The guilt lives in my hair.

The smiles and enthusiastic attitudes of my in-laws when they greet me make me want to gouge my eyeballs out with a dull spoon just to experience something less painful. When they hug me, I want to push them forcefully to the floor, stand above them, and scream, "Let's just all admit it! You fucking hate me for killing your son, so let's all just stop the fucking charade!"

I hate them for being nice to me, and I ache for their catastrophic loss, simultaneously and in equal measure.

As the drive continues, the kids are adding to my rising anxiety level. The closer we get, the harder it is to fight the frustrated tears. "Shut the fuck up!" I want to yell.

I don't want the kids anymore. I haven't wanted them for months. I admitted this out loud for the first time the other day to Veronica. She had no reaction to this other than to shake her head in nonjudgmental agreement. I, however, am judging myself. Years later, I will have the epiphany that the harshest judgments about my grief that I have ever received were from inside myself and fueled by the guilt I had to carry-and I *had* to carry it. People always talk about the stages of grief as if they are a choice-they aren't. They are things you have to fully experience, work through, and then validate before you can exist without them ruling your life. They never fully go away, and they only become manageable after the full weight of them has been felt. I don't know this today, though. Today all I can think about is how I want to leave my children on the side of the road, run away, fake my death, and move to a foreign country.

Parenting them is beyond my capabilities.

I can't raise them.

I can't answer any more of their questions about why John did this to them or to me.

I can't tuck them in at night and listen to their mindless storytelling.

I can't pray with them to a God I don't believe in anymore.

I can't comb their hair, cook their meals, or teach them about life when I haven't the slightest clue how to live it.

My kids are the things standing in the way of me and an endless stream of men and vodka. If I didn't have them, I could indulge in these things every night instead of only on the weekends. They are constant reminders of my moral decline, my substandard parenting, my guilt. I killed their father.

I have failed them.

I chose for them a father who cheated, lied, and abandoned them. I chose this life for them. A life they are being forced to bear through no fault of their own. They are so very innocent.

I have failed them.

As I continue the drive, I now have to hold back guilty tears in addition to the frustrated ones.

I should have never had children.

The mantra continues as I block out the kids' complaints and become hypnotized once again by the sound of the road. I've gotten so very good at checking out.

When we arrive at my in-laws', I am suppressing tears, and the kids are irritable from the long drive. My daughter snaps at me for locking the door before she's had a chance to get her stuffed animal out, and my son just rolls his eyes. I want to smack them both, hard.

One numb hour later, John's whole family is gathered in the dining room, about to begin the meal. "Let's all bow our heads to pray," my brother-in-law begins.

Now, in addition to the frustrated tears and the guilty tears, I will have to hold back the lonely tears—the sad, fat ones that threaten to leave my eyes each time I am in a situation like this when all around me, couples pair up like Noah's fucking ark, and I'm the dinosaur that got left behind. While I sit alone at the end of the kitchen island, pairs around the room hold hands to pray, declaring their ownership of each other, their fidelity and love. It's something John and I never had, not even when I thought things were good.

It is when I clasp my partner-free hands into my lap and close my eyes to diligently attempt to focus on something else—anything else—that I feel a gentle squeeze on my shoulder. I open my eyes to see Garrett standing above me with a close-mouthed grin, looking far too wise for his age.

Isabelle joins him and puts her hand on my other shoulder. I don't know what possessed them to do this. We were never much of a touchy-feely family. They had seemed so oblivious to my suffering, so why were they trying to comfort me? Then I had a heartbreaking thought: *Maybe they weren't*. Maybe *they* needed comfort. Maybe they, too, felt like dinosaurs as they saw everyone pairing off. Maybe they, too, felt like they had no one's hand to hold as they watched their cousins reach out for the hand of their own father.

I will spend the rest of this day combating the tears of complete and total shame. My children needed me, and I simply could not be there for them because I was so trapped inside my own pain.

I should have never had children.

I don't deserve them.

Chapter 9

I Pretend I Am Bold Like Lynnette

I look better in my white, off-the-shoulder, backless mermaid gown today than I did on my wedding day. Or maybe the full-length mirror in my bedroom closet in San Diego is just more flattering. Or maybe my veil is obstructing a more realistic view. Or maybe the third margarita is making me more optimistic. The reasons are not really important, though, because I believe myself to be luminous today!

Lynnette is luminous, too. She always is when she's pissed. She looks better in her strapless, empire-waist, ivory dress and veil than she did on her wedding day, in my opinion, mainly because she is not six months pregnant like she was when she originally wore it.

We are hauling her soon-to-be-ex's shit out of her house, so it'll be outside just in time for the rainstorm. Why? Because fuck him and his cheating, that's why. Also, fuck his beige and tan furniture; it's ugly. I'm moving into her house soon, and everything in my and Lynnette's new life will be cream, white, pink, and manless.

I pretend each one of Lynnette's ex's knickknacks (which I casually toss onto the lawn) belong to John and that I have been transported back to 2011, when I found out about his cheating. I pretend I handle his cheating the right way. With anger. With power. With ruining his precious possessions while wearing my wedding dress for all the neighbors to see. I pretend I am bold like Lynnette because in real life I wasn't, and I regret it.

Chapter 10

The Bomb Shelter

My children think I'm an idiot. Their arrogance about my intelligence began long before their teenage years. When my daughter was four years old and I brought her baby brother home from the hospital, she was irate at my inability to swaddle him properly. She insisted I take lessons from her and her baby doll, and lo and behold, in fifteen seconds flat, her doll swaddle was much more effective than my human-baby half-swaddle. Then there was the time my son had to teach me what an idiom was. He was in preschool.

The most obvious example, though, of my children's intellectual superiority over me happened on the morning after the discovery of Ho1's masturbation e-mails.

Isabelle's eyes were big and bright first thing that morning. Her brown, curly hair was in its usual tangled bedtime braid down the middle of her back. Even with summer coming to an end, her skin glowed bronze and pink in the natural sunlight of our kitchen. True to her eldest-sibling stereotype, my soon-to-be nine-year-old began to help me set the table and serve breakfast without being asked, probably because I wouldn't have done it to her standards anyway.

Garrett, on the other hand, entered the kitchen that morning with his usual scowl, the same one he would greet me with at his 2:00 a.m.

breastfeeding sessions when he was an infant. It was a look that said, "Listen, Mom, I've got to eat for biological purposes, but I don't have to like it." If not for his mismatched pajamas (Thomas the Tank Engine on top and Buzz Lightyear on the bottom) and his stuck-up dirty-blond hair—inherited from John—to balance out the dirty look on his face, he might be downright intimidating, even though he had just turned five years old a few weeks ago.

I had been awake for twenty-four hours; I looked like shit, and I felt like…whatever is worse than shit. It took every ounce of strength I could muster not to throw up the last remaining bits of stomach acid at the smell of the scrambled eggs and toast I was making. While my trembling hands prepared my cup of tea, images of the masturbation video mentally assaulted me without warning. I remember being cold—so very cold—in my very bones those first few months. That morning, in all my naiveté, I still thought hot tea would soothe me.

"Mom, I had the weirdest dream last night!" Isabelle started excitedly, after a few bites of toast. She was unusually bouncy that morning, which was strange to me because she, an empath like her mother, can so easily pick up on tension and moods. I thought for sure she'd pick up on the fact that her father was a cheating asshole, and her mother was a pathetic trauma victim and that she'd have a more somber disposition that morning.

"Oh yeah? What about, sweetie?"

"Our family was in a hole with the devil! Then he got outta the hole, and Daddy turned into God and was flying up in the sky, yelling at the devil to leave us all alone!" Her peppy tone suggested she was telling me a story about a trip to Disneyland.

Kids are creepy.

"Then Daddy said—"

I cut her off, saying, "Sweetie, was this a scary dream? I know if I dreamed about the devil, I'd feel scared."

She gave me a confused look and said, "No, it was a kinda silly dream, Mom."

"Oh, well, that's good. What did the devil look like?"

"Black with black wings," she said simply, and then went right back into her dream: "So then Daddy…but he wasn't Daddy, he was God, told us to start singing 'Happy Birthday,' and every time we sang, the devil got really mad!" She giggled and shoveled more food in her mouth. "So then, the hole we were in turned into our house, and the devil was there, too! And then there was a flood, and the house started filling up with water, and the devil was flying above us, trying to get the flood to stop. He was, like, trying to zap it with his fingers or something. But then he knew he couldn't stop the water, so he got mad and left, and then I woke up. Speaking of 'Happy Birthday,' make sure Namma makes my birthday cake double chocolate on Saturday."

If this had been a television show, I'd have dropped my teacup or spit the liquid out of my mouth, but this was real life, so I just stood in front of the stove and started at Belle like a lunatic.

"This dream wasn't scary for you at all?" I said after several seconds. "What about when the floodwaters were filling our house?"

"No, Mom, of course not!" she said with a laugh. "It's only the devil. God's more powerful…So you'll tell Namma about how I want chocolate on my cake?"

"I thought you said double chocolate," I teased, to keep the mood light and to not let on that I was freaked the fuck out.

"Make it triple!" Garrett chimed in. Just like clockwork, as soon as he was a few bites into his breakfast, he was back to his charming self.

"Mom, you look weird," Isabelle observed, not at all fooled by my attempt to appear nonchalant.

After breakfast, I walked Belle to her bedroom.

"So this dream," I said, "does Daddy come back from the sky?"

"No," she said, without inflection in her voice. When she shut her bedroom door, I crossed the hallway to the kid's bathroom, closed the door, and wept silently while hunched over the sink. I would graduate to bathroom floors in the near future, but on that day, it was the sink.

I allowed myself a whole minute to cry. A whole minute to consider the possibility that John would be leaving and not coming back. That the kids and I would one day be in rising floodwaters. And then, right at the sixty-second mark, I decided that everything was going to be just fine.

"It's not that bad. Marriages survive affairs every single day. John only had sex with one woman. This isn't that big of a deal," I told myself. "That dream was a good sign. It means that John is going to leave our family for a little bit, but it will be for the best. He'll turn into God—because, yeah, that happens—and save us from the hole and Satan!"

I didn't waste time on insignificant details like my daughter saying that he never came back…or the fact that John was an atheist.

I adore the denial stage of grief. I adore everything about it. The lies, the hope, the weight loss. Trauma victims: stay in denial as long as you possibly can. Ignore the signs. Ignore the flashing neon billboards that tell you the man you married is gone and won't be coming back. Coming out of denial is a lot like emerging from a bomb shelter during the apocalypse. You thought you hated the confined, dark space and bland food choices of the bomb shelter, so you emerge from it thinking, *Whatever is outside can't possibly be as bad as that bomb shelter*, and then you see the army of demons running at you with flaming pitchforks.

And so, during the first few months after John's affairs were revealed to me, I did what any self-respecting pacifist would do when presented with the fact that her marriage was over: I remained in the bomb shelter.

After this bathroom-sink crying sesh, I began a daily—sometimes hourly—ritual. I conjured up fond memories of John that proved he really was a swell guy. The "real" John would be returning to me soon, I convinced myself. I just needed to focus on the good times until then.

March 2004

I was twenty-one when I met John. He was nineteen. Tall, blond, lean, and with eyes that changed with the color of his clothes. They were at their best when he was shirtless and smiling. His thick-rimmed glasses looked out of place with his square jawline and commanding stature. Those ugly glasses were the first to go when we got married a year and a half later. It was obvious that he was still very much a kid by the way he was dressed, but there was something about him that seemed older. Mature.

I had to have him. And I did. Within thirty minutes of our first meeting at a party thrown in honor of my divorce from Isabelle's biological father, John and I were on the bathroom floor. We were also on the sink, and, OK, in the empty bathtub, too. I can't entirely blame this on the vodka or on my previous year of self-imposed celibacy. No, I knew it was love. I knew within moments of meeting him that I would marry him.

Chemistry is a funny thing. So unpredictable, so reckless.

April 2004

"Your brakes are squeaking," John said as he turned down the music on my car stereo.

"Yeah, I know. That's why I have the music up."

He playfully rolled his eyes. "Michelle, you can't just ignore it; you need new brake pads."

"No, right now I need to go to work."

"Quit both your jobs, and let me take care of you and the baby," he said…again. He'd been pleading with me since the second week after my divorce party to be his girlfriend. To let him be the man who saves me.

"You know I can't do that. I told you, this is just something I gotta do for me. You know I can't give that kind of power to a man again."

"I'm not him," he said with an edge in his voice that he always had when we talked about my ex-husband.

"I don't want to be late," I said, avoiding the topic altogether. We finished our lunch, and I dropped him back off at work. Eight hours later, I emerged from the back door of my night job to see a spotlight on my car. I couldn't make sense of what was happening until I saw John's unmistakable silhouette holding a tire.

"John? What are you doing?"

"Finishing your last brake pad," he said, as if I should have known.

And I knew at that moment that he'd take care of me and Belle forever.

May 2004

The first night John moved in to my apartment, I taught him Isabelle's bedtime routine: the bath temperature, the stories she liked to read, and the blankie she needed to hold. Before laying her in her crib each night, I showed him how I would hold her in my arms, sing her a particular lullaby, and say a prayer. Usually, she would stare up at me with wonder and peace. On that night, though, she couldn't take her eyes off John.

She was listening to my voice, but she was mesmerized by John. As I went to lay her down, she reached for him, grabbed onto his shirt with her tiny little fist, and wouldn't let go until he took her in his arms, kissed the top of her head, then laid her down.

As we crept out of her bedroom and closed the bedroom door behind us, John was grinning as he whispered, "Awwww, it was like she needed me. Did you see how she grabbed my shirt?" And instantly the three of us were a family, and John was a father.

May 2005

Dinnertime was chaos in our 950-square-foot apartment; the house was a mess, the TV was blaring, and a toddler was running around in her underwear while crying about something. Then the door handle rustled, and everything changed.

"Daddy's home!" I said to her enthusiastically.

"Daa-dee!" She ran her chubby two-year-old legs to the door and hopped in place, anticipating John's voice as if this weren't something she'd done every day for a year.

"There's my girl!" he said and swooped her up into his arms. He kissed me on the cheek and went to wash up. Before long, she was throwing a fit again, this time because a commercial was on and interrupting her Elmo marathon.

"John, can you handle her so that I can get dinner on the table?" I yelled down the hallway, irritated. "Joooohhhnnn?"

"Just a minute. I'm still washing up…Come here; I've got a surprise for you," he called to our daughter.

"What did you get her? She doesn't need any more toys. You know she has enough already!"

"Relax, woman. It's just a small little thing."

I heard him whispering to her, and her Elmo-induced fit subsided. "Piiiiiiitty!" I heard her say.

"Yes, pretty," he reinforced. "Now go show Mommy."

I was holding a saucepan with rice in the dining room. She entered with her little hand closed tight.

"Mommy, look at ta pitty!"

She opened her hand to reveal a ring: a three-stone diamond ring with a platinum band. I gasped. John peeked his head around the corner of the hallway. "Good girl," he said to her as she scampered off to go watch TV. Then he walked over to me, got down on one knee, and proposed.

I have no memory of what he said. I remember crying, and I remember the baby dancing around in the living room to the sound of Elmo, then running to me and saying, "Where's ta pitty? I want to hold it!"

Five months later, in a simple backyard wedding with ten guests, we were married.

November 2006

"I made him laugh! His first laugh ever…come see!" John said. Isabelle and I left our half-eaten plates at the dinner table to see our new baby boy lying on his back in the crib, staring up at John.

"Watch…" John commanded. As he started to remove Garrett's onesie, John's calloused hands lightly brushed against Garrett's sensitive torso, and he let out the most heartwarming giggle imaginable. He and John didn't take their eyes off each other the whole time.

May 2007

Everything at our new house would have been perfect, if it weren't for the portable toilet in the front yard. When I called several times over the first month after we moved in, no one would claim it. The toilet company would blame the construction company, and the construction company would tell me it was the toilet company's responsibility. We were having a housewarming barbecue that weekend, and I couldn't stand the thought of our guests having to park next to a smelly portable toilet.

When John made his daily call home on his lunch break that Friday afternoon, the stress of putting on a housewarming party with a four-year-old, eight-month-old, and a portable toilet was just too much. I was practically in tears over that stupid toilet when I answered the phone.

"I'll handle it," he said. Sixty minutes later, John was home from work early and on his Quad. He attached a combination of tie-downs, ratchet straps, and rope from the toilet to the back of the quad. Garrett wouldn't stop screaming, and Belle was covered in sand. He motioned to me to hand him the screaming baby.

Garrett quieted down immediately at the vibrations of the quad. John hit the gas, and Belle and I stared in amazement as John's quad actually began to drag the toilet.

"Go, Daddy, go!" Belle cheered, and I just started laughing. He hauled it out to the highway, removed the tangle of straps, and rode the quad back with Garrett still in his lap.

The housewarming barbecue was a success.

How did John go from this man to the man holding a gun to his torso at 9:00 p.m. on a Sunday? I still don't know.

Chapter 11

From John's Blog: Goodbye

February 6, 2014 forty-six days before his suicide
Normally when someone dies you hear speeches about how great they were and how much of an influence in your life they have been. What if the person is hated? Well the same thing normally happens. I'm gonna break this trend on me right now because I have died, at least the old me.

John was a person on this earth. He consumed oxygen and used up natural resources with no regard to anything else. He was not productive to the advancement of the species and only had negative impacts on everyone and everything around him.

He left behind two beautiful children and a loving wife who were forever impacted by his bad choices. He thought of himself as a caring loving person who was good. But he was very wrong. I hate him. He was an evil person who only cared for himself and never stopped to think what he was doing to people around him. He was addicted to pornography and addicted to himself. This caused him to loose the people most important in his life for a ridiculous obsession like naked women. How ridiculous. How could you have called yourself a good person? How could you even look in the mirror and think to yourself that you looked good? Did you not see the evil in your heart? I don't think you did. Your ugliness was hiding behind your pride, ego, and selfishness. How dare you!

I will not be missing anything about you because even your "good" deeds were ways to try to feel better about who you were. You were feeling guilt without even noticing. Well now we all know. And we were sick of you anyways. And you don't need to take my word on this, just look at how many people you drove out of your life. Your kids, your wife, and the rest of your family all don't want to be around you. And now we are morning your death? We should be celebrating because you will never be welcome back in this world and you would never be wanted back in this world.

Although some of your secrets will never be told because of the pain it would cause, some will come out right now.

You were addicted to pornography since 13. You cheated on your wife continuously throughout the marriage. You sent naked pictures to multiple women. You lost jobs for being late because you couldn't control your sex addiction. You lost friends because of your sex addiction. You lost beautiful girlfriends because of your sex addiction. You were angry and not supportive of your children. You cheated on them too! You lied, cheated and stole from people. You did everything possible to be a horrible person. And I, for one, am very glad you are gone forever. You will never hurt another soul again. Thank you for dying!

Now that the old me is dead and my pain is out and I have said my goodbyes, I now have closure on my past so I can move onto the more important future. Let the healing and rebuilding gates open to my better future and hope that I am strong enough to allow the changes.

If mental illness is the seed of suicide, then self-hatred is the roots, and lies are the water. When John died, self-hatred was passed on to me.

Chapter 12

How to Drop the Widow Bomb on Your Date in Three Easy Steps

Step 1: The Build

First and foremost, on dates, act like you are normal. I know this can be difficult, but with a little bit of alcohol and a quick chant at the foot of your Beyoncé altar, anything is possible.

The detonation of the widow bomb is all about the timing. One must build up to the explosion as slowly as possibly in order to achieve the greatest level of personal satisfaction upon detonation…and we'd all be lying if we didn't admit that there is indeed a level of satisfaction upon seeing the horrified look on people's faces when we tell them we are widowed.

During small talk with your unsuspecting date, at all costs, avoid your marital status. Change the subject. People love to talk about themselves, so redirect any and all personal questions back to your date.

Example (this may or may not be a true story of something that actually happened to me):

HIM: So how long have you been divorced?
YOU: I'm not divorced. This wine is really good! How's your beer?
HIM: Good. So you never married your kids' father?

YOU: Yes, we were married for eight years.
HIM: Oh, so you guys are like, separated?
YOU: I suppose you could say that. What is your favorite sexual position, so I know for later?

Sidenote—the sex-position question has a 95 percent success rate for complete and total distraction until you start taking each other's clothing off. At this point, your date will press you for more details on the whereabouts of your "separated" spouse to ensure that he or she will not be coming through the door in a jealous rage to attack.

Sidenote two—naked time is by far the most fun time to drop the widow bomb, so please use this strategy every chance you get.

Sidenote three—the only time the sexual-position question won't work is if you unknowingly find yourself on a date with a pastor (trust me on this one).

Step 2: The Climax

Now for the fun! Make sure you are face to face when the big moment presents itself, as the look on the face of your date is half the fun! If it is a man and he is already naked, all the better, as you will get to see more than just their face turn into a frown (trust me on this one, too).

There are several different phrases you can use. I keep a list of these phrases on a poster in my room and check them off after each date to make sure I use all of them equally. I'm a huge advocate for equality in all forms.

The cute approach: "I'm widowed, but it's fine because I get to wear a really cute black veil anytime I want, and I have a standing prescription for Valium. If you ever want me to share, I totally will."

The practical approach: "He's dead, but this works out for you because you don't ever have to worry about me going back to him."

The (slightly) psychotic approach: "He offed himself after cheating on me for seven years, and I'm really angry, which means the sex we are about to have will be so hot."

The "victim" approach: If at any point you change your mind about wanting to have sexy time with your date, just simply say, "I'm widowed," and then cry until your partner starts giving you food and/or money to make you stop weeping while he calls you a taxi.

Step 3: The Recovery

Once the victim, I mean your date, has been completely turned off and repulsed by you because that person is emotionally ill-equipped to deal with your life, make sure you comfort him or her. With a punch in the face.

If someone cannot see that your Widow Badge is something that indicates strength, empathy, and a unique view on life, that person deserves to be punched. Your Widow Badge is not something many people will appreciate. How sad for them, because they are missing an opportunity to love someone whose well of compassion is as deep as her craziness is vast.

The dates who reject you are missing out on getting to know someone who spontaneously dances in the grocery store and flips off strangers, all in the name of expressing her inability to care what others think of her. They are giving up the opportunity of 2:00 a.m. chats with someone who can teach them things about life that no one else knows until they have joined the widowhood. Yes, how sad for *them* indeed.

And lastly, in the recovery process, comfort yourself after these train wreck dates with a slice of chocolate pie and a group of widow friends who just *get it*.

Chapter 13

The Tiny Fragments

John always did Halloween well. He did two costumes every year: one to match me for the adult parties we went to and one to match the kids' costumes when we took them trick-or-treating. I never cared to partake in this free-candy-athon or to dress up with the kids. I'd always stand back on sidewalks and street corners, pretending to take pictures with my phone when, truth be told, I was really just playing on social media.

Don't judge. You parents out there know that these kid-centered holiday rituals are boring as hell.

If John was bored by this ritual, though, he never let on; he'd walk hand in hand with our son and daughter to each door, being particularly sensitive as to whether or not the surroundings were too frightening. If they were, he'd decide if he should carry them or just take the kids to a different house altogether.

With an uncharacteristic patience, he'd teach them how to collect treats at each door, when the shock of getting free candy while playing dress-up still paralyzed the kids as preschoolers. He'd of course collect candy for himself, and every year, without complaint, he'd give me all the chocolate he had earned. He knew I loved chocolate, and I knew he loved me.

I miss believing that lie. Now I don't know what to believe. Did he ever love me? Did I ever really know him? Why did he do this to our children? Was it really my fault, like he'd said in his suicide note?

I am in my bathroom, recalling the memory of John at Halloween to erase the anger rising up in me, so I will be able to sleep at least a few consecutive hours tonight. The only problem with removing the anger, though, is that it will inevitably be replaced by sadness, and sadness makes me sleep for days. Which is worse: no sleep, or too much? Shaking with rage all night, or being comatose from the pain of good memories?

I want to be drunk, but I can't be tonight, so I will be full. I am ravenously eating all the chocolate I have just stolen from the kids' glow-in-the-dark candy sacks, hoping by some miracle they won't notice tomorrow morning.

OK, fine, you can judge me now.

I couldn't walk my son and daughter to the doors tonight like their dad had once done. I am not ready to fill his shoes. I am too weak, too broken. Too checked out. I left the task of door-to-door candy fetching to the grandparents, who are also broken beyond measure but somehow seem stronger than me.

Everyone seems stronger than me.

The rubber strings of those flimsy dollar-store Halloween masks that walked by me all night seemed stronger than me. I am in pieces. Small, insignificant fragments.

Garrett walks into my bathroom without knocking. His mask is off, but he's still wearing the clothes of his Minecraft character. I panic that he will see the Kit Kat bar I am hoarding, so I start shoving it into the pockets of my skinny jeans like the good little chocolate junkie I am. He looks sick.

"What's wrong, buddy? Got a tummy ache from all the candy?"

"No," he says with an uncertainty in his voice and his shoulders slumped down. "I think I'm sad."

"Really? About what?"

"I think…" And then his little chin begins to quiver, and his face begins to contort, like it did when he would hold funerals in the backyard for his dead tomato worms as a kindergartner. "I think I am just missing Daddy," he confesses, and the tears stream down his baby face.

This is only the third time he's ever cried over his dad.

I close the toilet lid, sit, and offer him my lap. He lets me cradle him like a baby. *How long has it been since I've held my son like this? Will it be the last time?*

"Daddy was always so much fun on Halloween, wasn't he?" I say, without any tears of my own.

"Uh-huh," he says and then cries some more. "Mom, I don't want this to make you sad, but I have to tell you something, OK?"

"OK, just say what you need to say, buddy. I'll be just fine," I reply.

As if I have a choice.

"I just really miss Daddy because he was my favorite, and I…I just liked him more than I like you…and…I think about how if you would've died and not Daddy, then I wouldn't be the only boy in this house." He nervously looks at my face for a reaction. His uncertainty makes me feel an unspeakable tenderness toward him.

"That's true," I say softly. He relaxes. I continue, "Daddy always did more fun things with you than Mommy did, and it must be lonely to be the only boy in the house." I surprise myself with this empathetic statement. I silently wonder why his proclamation didn't obliterate the tiny fragments that are left of me. John was his favorite. He wishes I were dead instead of his father.

I feel helpless as Garrett cries harder. His tears and snot are running down my arm as I hold him. There are no words to say, so I resort to primal motherly sounds of comfort, while brushing the hair from his forehead with my fingertips.

My sounds are worthless; he only cries harder. I go silent, resigned to the fact that all I can do is rock him.

He cries louder, with moans and shutters and deep, staccato chest heaves.

I sway my body back and forth even though he is eight years old and so big and awkward in my arms that I hurt. I sway even though the chocolate in my pocket is being melted. I sway even though I know I am powerless against his pain and longing and confusion. I just sway.

After several minutes, he gradually sits up, uses my sleeve as a tissue, and says, "I'm gonna go to bed now, Mom. Thanks." He leaves after a brief hug, as if nothing had happened. My arm begins to tingle as the blood rushes back into it.

I cry about his pain when his footsteps are out of earshot. I cry about how I just spent Halloween with my own father walking next to me, and my children won't ever do that again. I cry about all the things Garrett will want his father present for and how those desires will never be met. I cry about my fragility and then about the guilt over allowing myself to be so fragile. I cry that I was too weak to escort my children to houses tonight. I cry because I cannot get the semimelted Kit Kat bar out of my pants pocket, and I *need* chocolate.

Chocolate will fix everything. I take off my pants…Just keep on judging me.

While prying the shiny red wrapper out of my pocket, I begin to smile. At first it is at the ridiculousness of me standing in my bathroom in my underwear trying to salvage the last bits of chocolate and wafer from my ruined, too-tight pants. Then my smile turns into a grin, and my grin turns into a laugh. I am laughing at myself, and then, I am laughing at myself for laughing at myself. Then I am crying again, only to be interrupted by more fits of my own laughter.

I am really cracking up, I think, as I lick the chocolate from my fingers.

How can I possibly be laughing after what my son just said to me? I pull myself together and replay his words. *I just really miss Daddy because he was my favorite, and I…I just liked him more than I like you…*

He knew his comment had the potential to hurt me, but he said it anyway. He was not trying to be rude or hurtful. It was just simply his truth, and for some reason, he knew he could speak this truth openly with me.

It was as if he didn't know how delicate I am. It was as if he thought I was dependable and comforting. It was as if he thought I was easy to talk to. It was as if he thought the tiny fragments that are left of me are strong, and if he thinks all these things about me, they must be true.

Chapter 14

Not a Widow

My need for the "widow card" joke began at the gynecologist's office, a month after John's death. I was mindlessly filling out paperwork in a waiting room filled with mostly couples—women with budding baby bumps and men rushing to get them water before sitting down, casually sliding their arms around the soon-to-be mothers. I remember when that used to be my life. Now my life has been reduced to the marital-status box on the paperwork in front of me: single, married, divorced, widowed.

Widowed. I couldn't possibly check the "widowed" box, could I? Am I a *widow*? I didn't feel like a widow. I'm only thirty-one years old, not to mention John and I were separated when he died—does this count? A widow is sad. I was not; my life had been a nonstop anxiety-fueled episode of *The Bachelorette* mixed with the Home Shopping Network since he died. Sure I had cried, but they were tears for my children and John's family. I didn't have the right to miss him, to cry for him, or to mourn him. I am the reason he is dead; he committed suicide because of my refusal to stay with him. *I don't get to be a widow.*

I look at the patient-admission forms in my lap and decide to check the "widowed" box. Maybe the doctor will be sympathetic when I answer the dreaded, "How many sexual partners have you had in the last ninety days?" question, if she knows I am a recent widow. Maybe my widow status will make her assume I'm too fragile for her to lecture me on safe-sex practices, and I can avoid her judgment altogether.

My widow status works. In lieu of a raised eyebrow or free condom offer, I receive her condolences after she finishes the exam and goes over paperwork with me. "It must be difficult to lose someone you love, especially someone you've had children with." She waits for my response.

"Thank you," is all I say. Can she tell that I don't miss him? Can she tell I've been so embittered by the infidelities committed by him before his death that I haven't cried over him?

For the two months following that day, I receive condolences everywhere I go. Life in a small town is like that. Everyone wants to share fond memories of John—the John they knew in high school or middle school, the John they knew at work. With each commiseration, my guilt increases. Why are they telling me these stories? I am not John's widow! I don't want to hear good things about him!

I want to hold on to the bad things. I want to cling to the times his eyes emptied, as his voice rose along with his temper, without warning. I want to clutch the way his apathy invalidated me when I needed validation the most after his affairs. I want to latch on to thoughts of him demoting me to a paper doll by choosing my clothing each day; I want to wear the humiliation of this memory, in particular, like a fur coat in August. These things make it easy for me to hate him. These things keep me from missing him. I want to think of him as inhuman and selfish instead of an admirable man who eventually succumbed to a brain chemistry he had no control over. I don't deserve to be called a widow.

I decide to cope with my guilt about the undeserved sympathies I receive by turning my faux widow status into a joke that my best friend Lynnette and I call "the widow card." When she asks me to do something simple, like hand her a drink, I respond with, "But I can't! I'm a *widow*!" We both laugh, and then she reminds me that she's only letting me use the widow-card excuse for one year before she stops waiting on me hand and foot.

My refusal to cry over John, and the widow-card joke, sustains me for one more month. I fill this month with dirty martinis at first and then with slightly dirty martinis. One morning I decide that martini glasses are much too small for olives, so I forgo them. That night I graduate to straight vodka. Beautiful vodka, whose clarity looks so much like a million-dollar diamond that I begin to believe I am a diamond, too, just by ingesting it. I am unbreakable. The only problem with being vodka, though, is that men will find you irresistible, and by irresistible, I mean vulnerable. I add men to my daily vodka regime because I can. Straight up, on the rocks, extra dirty—I add them all. Then one morning I wake up on a man's brown leather couch to realize the entire month of May has passed and parts of June. I realize it is the day John's ashes are to be buried.

The cemetery was abandoned on that hot day in mid-June. Even the birds had deemed it too uncomfortable to make their presence known verbally. I was asked by John's family to bring something to put in the burial box that encased his urn before it was lowered into the ground. I declined. His burial box should include things from his family, of which I was no longer a part. I do not get to do the sentimental things widows do. I don't get to be a widow.

My young friend Allyssa gets to be a widow. Her husband, Jeff, was buried ten feet away from where I am now sitting, almost a year ago. Jeff passed away suddenly of a natural illness at the age of twenty-six. Allyssa loved her husband, and he loved her, and they loved their babies. They loved each other in a way only people in their twenties know how to love: with passion, lack of inhibition, and purpose. We lose this as we enter our thirties.

Thirtysomethings love with repetition, familiarity, and a sense of duty. In many ways, true love only exists between people in their twenties. Love in our twenties happens before the realization that bonds and promises can be broken. Love in our twenties happens before our naked bodies age and become something we only want seen in the dark. Love in our twenties happens before we are taught that codependency is a bad thing. Jeff and Allyssa loved each other in their twenties.

I remember watching Allyssa's children put handfuls of dirt on their daddy's coffin as it was lowered. I remember wondering how she was able to stand upright. I remember feeling guilty that I could relate to her despair through my experiences with John's adultery. How could I possibly compare her loving, devoted husband's tragic death to my husband breaking his vows of fidelity to me? The two are not the same.

As John's ashes begin their descent into the clay earth, the tears of my children sitting in my lap flow freely, and for the first time since his death, it occurs to me that John no longer has a body. John is ash. His entire being is now encapsulated by a small, fabricated box. As I fix my eyes on the dull metal, I begin to meditate on thoughts of his body. His body, which I once regarded as part of my own, is now reduced to dust. I will never see his body again.

I flash back to two and a half years ago, after my discovery of his first affair. John had moved all his things into the detached garage that was built on the back part of our property. The detachment and dust of that garage was a perfect metaphor for who he'd become in the last few years.

He was sitting in a folding chair next to an engine from one of his many unfinished car projects, staring absently past me as I paced. I was openly sobbing and asking him why he'd given his body to another. He wouldn't answer me. I walked over and knelt in front of him. My knees, bare from my cutoff shorts, instantly became coated in dirt and engine grease. I didn't care. When I lay my head on his lap, his arms went from crossed in front of his chest to limp on either side of him. His torso, neck, and head arched away from me in disgust at my pathetic display of grief.

I took his hands and made them cup my wet, salty face. "Your hands," I had sobbed, "your hands were on her. *These hands*, my hands." He nodded his head in agreement, not once looking down upon me. When I let go of his lifeless, heavy hands, they dropped back to his sides. I then crawled into his lap and placed my hands on the part of his neck that merged into his shoulder.

"She was here, too?" He nodded in agreement. "And here?" I asked with snot puddling on my upper lip as I let my hands glide over his chest and abdomen. He nodded, still cold and lifeless. "Say something to me!"

I shook him. "How can you do this to me?"

He looked down on me, and without inflection in his voice, he said, "I do not love you. I never did. All these years, I was only playing house. I knew you'd be a good mom, and women like her are not, but I love her. I want to be with her, not you."

There was something that burst inside me. It was a feeling that rippled from my esophagus to the ends of each strand of my hair and down to my toes. The feeling died down quickly to make room for the fear that I felt next. It was oppressive, demonic, and all consuming. The fear took root as I looked at John. The cloudiness of his eyes as he spoke those words to me obliterated the last seven years of my life. The fear manifested in my lungs; it took my breath, causing violent fits of coughing and gasping between my sobs. This fear would continue to take things from me in the years to come, things like my sleep, my appetite, and my faith.

I didn't know until that moment how much I had loved John. I didn't realize until then how much of myself I had sacrificed at the altar. These things had been immeasurable until their absence. I had been in love with a figment of my imagination, devoted to a man who never existed. I wished for a grave site or some sort of ceremony to help me accept that fact that the man I had devoted my life to no longer existed.

My weight plummeted. I wore sunglasses and no makeup to work. My menstrual periods ceased for three cycles. I started losing chunks of my hair. I vomited so frequently that my teeth became loose from the stomach acid. I was hospitalized for heart problems and fainting spells. I began taking pills: huge, coated, colorful antidepressants that took away my ability to write and to feel.

It is possible to mourn the living. I didn't know yet that his erratic and cruel behavior was a symptom of his declining mental health; I wouldn't know this until long after his suicide. All I knew was that the tender, lively man I had married six years ago was gone, and my mourning of him began on that day, two and a half years before his death.

When the last bits of earth were shoveled over John's urn at his funeral, I realized I finally had what I'd wished for: a place to grieve him. I publicly wept over the death of my husband. A death that had taken place in our garage years ago. For the first time, I cried for his physical death and for the hope I'd harbored that we would get back together one day.

Chapter 15

What I Told My Children about Their Father's Suicide

*F*irst, a disclaimer: I am not a doctor or therapist of any kind. Deciding what you tell *your* children about suicide or the death of their parent is entirely up to *you*. What you decide to tell or not tell them is about knowing who they are and what they can and cannot handle based on their unique personalities. The night my husband killed himself, I called our marriage counselor and discussed with him the best way to tell my children what had happened. The following chapter is about the conversation I had with my kids (to the best of my memory), and is being published with the intent to help others, not to judge what methods anyone else has used in regards to their children's grief processes.

The transcript of the conversation I had with my kids about John's death is being shared with the permission of my children (now eleven and fifteen years old). Certain parts that they found too personal have been left out, but the majority of the full conversation I had with them has remained intact.

I believe talking to children about the death of a parent should never be a onetime conversation. I believe it should be a series of discussions that take place throughout their lifetimes, and the following blog post was the first of those conversations.

The "S" Word

I remember when I thought the most uncomfortable conversation I'd have with my children was about sex; turns out, I was wrong. John's suicide in 2014 obliterated my fear of the sex talk; actually, his suicide pretty much obliterated everything in my life...and all the things around my life.

And outside of my life.

And inside of my body, heart, and soul.

Ah, suicide aftermath! The horrible gift that keeps on giving.

Why I Chose to Tell Them the Truth

I want all of you to know why I decided to tell my kids the truth about John's suicide in the first place. I mean, I could've spared them the trauma of suicide aftermath and told him he accidentally shot himself during target practice, right?

Wrong. For our family, this would've been the wrong choice.

What I know about my son (who was seven years old at the time) is that he is curious, and what I know about my daughter (who was eleven at the time) is that she is highly intuitive, which is why there was no way in hell I could've lied to them about their father's suicide. Not only was the term "self-inflicted" going to be on his death certificate (that they would be able to have access to one day should they ever want it), but I also knew that they would be able to tell that I was hiding something from them.

I feel like, in general, we as a society tend to minimize not only the intelligence of children, but the deeply profound spiritual connection they have to their parents.

Kids know.

Kids know more than we think, so I believe that we might as well tell them. My six years of working with elementary and middle school special-needs students in addition to parenting my own children has assured me of this fact.

Kids know.

I feel like lying to my children would've invalidated their inner voices. It would've invalidated the thing whispering to them, "There's something more to this story…" and as their mother, I've always believed it is one of my many jobs to teach them to not only listen to their inner voices, but to also trust those inner voices.

I felt completely confident telling them the facts about what had happened in short, easy-to-understand sentences. I told them a few facts that morning and answered any questions they had, while restraining (by some miracle) panic in my voice.

Shock is a gift, and it's what made me able to tell my kids what had happened without having my emotions usurp their own.

What I Told Them

> Setting: In their bedroom at my parents' house, early Monday morning
> ME: We need to talk. Last night, while you were sleeping, Daddy died.
> THEM: (*cry hysterically*)
> ME: (*physically comforts them without saying a word*)
> THEM: How did he die?
> ME: His brain was sick.
> THEM: We saw him yesterday, and he didn't seem sick.
> ME: Brain sickness can be hard for other people to see. I think he hid it from us so that we didn't worry.
> THEM: Did he just fall down, and then you took him to the hospital?
> ME: No. He died out in the middle of the desert.

THEM: How did you know he died?

ME: He knew he was going to die, so he sent me a text message, and then I called him and talked to him for a little bit before he died while Papa called 911. But by the time they found Daddy, he was already dead.

THEM: How did he know he was going to die? Did his brain just start hurting?

ME: Daddy did something called "suicide." His brain was so sick that it told him he shouldn't be alive anymore. His brain told him to take a gun out to the desert and to shoot himself.

THEM: He shot himself?

ME: Yes. But it wasn't him shooting himself. It was his sick brain. If your heart stops working, you have a heart attack. If your lungs stop working, you can't breathe, and you die. If your brain stops working, it controls your thoughts, and your thoughts tell you that you should be dead, so you do whatever you can to make yourself die.

THEM: (*crying more*)

ME: There is going to be a lot happening this week. There is already family in the living room, and more people might want to come by to see us. You guys can do and say and feel whatever you want. If you don't want people here, I'll tell them to leave. If you want your friends here and want to stay in your room, that's OK, too. Nothing you do will get you into trouble except for maybe if you burn the house down (*slight laughter and ease of tension*). You don't have to go to school this week unless you want to. You might hear people using phrases like "passed away, funeral, casket, suicide, cremation," and other things that sound confusing. If you want to know what they mean, just ask me. If you have any other questions about what happened, just ask me. You will see a lot of adults cry. This might feel scary for you, but it's going to be OK. A sad thing happened, and it's OK for everyone to be sad and cry.

And just like that, their innocence was taken.

So many parents miss this. They wake up one morning to find that their children no longer exist in the realm of childhood, and they wonder when and how it happened. I got to witness the beginning of my children's transformation into the heaviness of adulthood. They had responsibility now. They would have to learn to heal themselves. This is something I cannot do for them; this is something that cannot be taught.

I don't remember if it was seconds or minutes, but that morning before I told them, in the presence of that unique kind of light that happens when it is still nighttime, but also morning, I watched my kids sleep. I watched and savored their last moments as children before I had to teach them the one universal truth about life: that it is not fair. Dads die.

There will never be a greater privilege in my life than watching the last moments of their childhood.

And even with all the darkness that took place after this, even after all the screams and tears and coldness inside my body that I still can't seem to shake, this memory of them sleeping warms me.

Chapter 16

September Rain

I just wanted that night to be over. The party, the pit in my stomach, the September rain, the lies. It was the first and only time I would see my husband drunk, and he was terrifying. Not in a way you'd imagine, though—he wasn't yelling or cursing or throwing things, he was simply distant, and this space terrified me.

Along with his distance, he was also lively, jovial, and just so…so… whatever the word is that means you no longer give a shit about your wife. He was that.

He openly groped women's asses, posed for pictures with their breasts, and challenged everyone to shot-drinking contests while looking over his shoulder to make sure I was witnessing every part of it.

He had hated me for months, maybe even years, and he was done suppressing it.

I deserved this, and we both knew it. I had the audacity to love him unconditionally as his maltreatment of me increased, and he hated me for this and for all the other things he was incapable of doing that I could do with such ease. I could hope, I could see light, I could…be intimate. Yes, I could be intimate, and he could not, and he was done being reminded of this.

"Leave me," he continually challenged me, in between shots of tequila and laughter with women who refused to acknowledge me.

Still I stayed. I stayed through the freak desert rainstorm. I stayed through him and his married girlfriend singing Carrie Underwood's "Before He Cheats," on the karaoke machine…Fuck that song, by the way…I stayed for the police coming to shut things down. I stayed when he told me he wanted a divorce just before he got into her car.

I stayed for 870 more days.

I used to be embarrassed by this, but now I am proud, not of my martyrdom, but of my tenacity.

I used to think he was just cruel, but now I know he was sick; his suicide would be proof of that.

I used to think one day I would heal, but now I know I won't.

Wounds close, and then they reopen. They never really go away when you are someone like me. I don't forgive. I don't let go. I don't move on. I don't get over. Maybe this is a choice…I don't know. Maybe enough time hasn't passed…I don't know that, either.

Chapter 17

A Hammer

I am mad. I mean mad in both definitions of the word: crazy and angry. I am mad. It is 1:00 a.m., and I wake up, shaking with rage. I can't pinpoint my trigger. Is it my dead husband showing up in my dreams, refusing to fight with me as I throw wine bottles at him? Is it that yesterday I finished yet another Christian self-help bullshit book that once again brought me no relief? Is it that I ended things with Chad because I was starting to have feelings for him, and he let me go without so much as a hesitation? Is it that I saw Ho1 at a school function the other night with her family still intact, posing for family pictures? So much to choose from…My anger doesn't waste much time trying to figure out the root of things; my anger just reacts. My anger hands me a hammer.

The neighbor's dog won't stop barking at me, but I don't care. Walking next door to my house (which I still can't bring myself to enter) and taking a hammer to that railroad tie John was supposed to use to build our fence six years ago (but couldn't find the time because he had so many women to keep up with) is better than the two martinis I had last night, and that is saying a lot because I love martinis.

My arms are burning, and it's not long before the tears of fury are running down my neck and soaking into my shirt and bathrobe. *"Fuck you, John,"* I keep chanting over and over again in a rhythm. *"Fuck you, God."*

I only decide to stop when the friction of the tool and my wedding ring (that I dug out of the safe and wore last night to bed as I cried myself to sleep) causes a blister on my finger that ruptures after an hour and a half. My ring finger swells, and now I can't get my stupid rings off.

I walk back in the pitch black of the early morning hours to my parents' house. Once inside, I don't go back to sleep. My rage will never be satiated. I cannot fight with John. I'll never be able to yell at him, curse at him, and punch him in the face. I will never get the apology I deserve from him or from all the "hers." I will never know all the lies he told me. I will spend the rest of my life not having any outlet for my hatred. Or will I? Around sunrise, I must have subconsciously decided that a great way to express my rage is through sex because somehow I end up having sex pretty much every single day in a row for months after this, and it brings me more relief than anything I have ever read, prayed, or ingested. I have been told this is not a healthy expression of my anger; I've never been very interested in healthy living anyway. It bores me.

Chapter 18

From John's Blog: Battling Demons

February 10, 2014 forty-two days before his suicide

Something about me you don't know yet is I am an atheist. I have called out to god in the past and haven't gotten any response. I have a hard time believing in something I can't see hear or touch. But on the flip side I do believe in love. Love is not something that can be understood. You can't touch, hear or see it but I know it is there because I feel it. So the other day I called out to god for help. The only thing that could fix us now is a miracle and I will try anything. So as I called out to god I thought about everything that I have done wrong in the marriage. The lying, cheating, and mis trust. And thought to myself why would I deserve someone so great?

Funny thing happened. I broke down and started crying hysterically. I don't know if it was a sign or it was hopelessness. But I never cry. And I mean never. Now I can't stop. A sad song plays on the radio and I have to pull over. I think about what my kids are going through, I can't get off the bed. I think about loosing my wife and I can't breathe. I have become an emotional wreck. Is this because I asked for help? Is it because my walls are finally down? Is it a divine intervention? I don't know.

But I am starting to understand why people believe in god. And that is because when things become out of control there is no stopping it. There is no way to fully prepare yourself for every good or bad experience in your life. I guess the only real way to prepare yourself is to have a blanket answer for everything that is good or bad in your life. And I think the answer is trust in him and he shall set you free. Free from worries, timelines or agendas that bound this physical world to itself.

Is there something more out there? Is there a god? I don't know yet but if he is out there man I could use his help right now. Help me make the choices that are best for the family. Help me be the man that I want to be. Help my children when they are in need. And help my wife through her struggles. Of course crying as I am writing this.

Just help. Please. I am ready to believe if you can help me through this struggle

Chapter 19

The Anger Orgasm

The best part about John's affairs was the shopping. It was all pretty much downhill after that.

It is December of 2011, and according to the scale this morning, I have dropped thirty pounds since opening the vulva video e-mails from my husband's girlfriend two months ago. *My husband's girlfriend…*feel free to read that last sentence as many times as you need to for the horror to sink in.

I am in desperate need of work pants that aren't being folded over and pinned to keep from falling off my slender hips. Buying a few pairs of slacks feels so good that I go back the next day for shoes and then accessories.

It's kind of a blur after that.

When I get home from shopping, I flaunt my new possessions in front of my apathetic, wayward husband. He refuses to give me the satisfaction of acknowledging my treasures, but I flaunt them anyway and relish in the deliverance of my anger. Anger is too trite of a word…Let's go with the term "murderous rage," shall we? Yes, shopping and flaunting releases the murderous rage that lives in me without risking jail time for assault…OK, homicide.

Our marriage counselor calls my shopping "avoidance" and "passive-aggressive." I call it "having an anger orgasm."

Sure, I could've orgasmed in other ways, like, oh, I don't know… yelling at John? Telling him how much he had devastated me? Venting to my friends? But no. It was decided early on by my Bible and me that suppressing my murderous rage around John was in our best interest…you know, turn the other cheek and all that shit. Plus, he often reminded me that if I so much as raised my voice to him, told anyone, or tried to make him feel bad about what he had done, he would divorce me, but that is an entirely different story altogether…a different story and a different Michelle.

Thank God for shopping, or I would have killed him.

After I made him watch his whores burn to death at the stake.

The stake that was attached to his precious Cadillac.

That was also on fire.

From matches that I bought using the money he had hidden from me in his garage.

What were we talking about again? Oh yes, shopping!

The next day, I shop again. I turn up the heat after John once again refuses to acknowledge my newest pair of slouchy leather stiletto boots by causally mentioning how we won't be making his car payment this month because I spent it at the outlet mall.

Mission accomplished—he is furious. My rage has turned into power.

I pour gasoline on the flames by refusing to engage in an argument about my spending. I just quietly justify my boot purchases by telling him they are work related (because everyone who works with special-needs children at an elementary school needs stiletto boots), and we can write them off on our taxes this year…if only I can find those pesky receipts, darn it! Then I use my "all this stress from your cheating has just made me lose so much weight so quickly, and even my feet have shrunk" martyrdom to exhaust him until he retreats to the garage.

His fury about my spending catapults me from the economical clearance rack to the full-price new-arrivals rack in every store I enter for the next five days in a row. I feel power infusing my body after it enters through my fingertips with each item of clothing I touch. The power John and his whores took from me returns in the form of cotton, wool, suede, leather, and cashmere. The power continues its take-over with each *ding* of the cash register as my rage is simultaneously expelled.

For the first time in months, I feel like I am exhaling.

As I carelessly add raincoats (we live in the bone-dry Mojave Desert) and snow boots (we seriously live in the Mohave Desert) to my shopping cart, I remind myself of the $500-a-month car bill John had incurred *without my permission* six months ago as a result of his penis convincing him that Hol's bare ass on the leather seat of a 2011 Cadillac would satisfy his latest sexual fantasy.

Yes, please, I'll take that raincoat in purple and in zebra print, too.

Day four of my shopping spree begins a three-day stretch of nothing but dress shopping. I even, to the shock of my coworkers, call in sick to work for the first time in three years.

Are you really sick? they ask.

No, I am finally well, I respond.

I need dresses. I need them like I need validation. I need cocktail dresses for all the future cocktail parties that maybe might possibly happen. I need prom dresses because I could one day be invited to a quinceañera. I need sun dresses, just in case we have a heat wave in December. I need church dresses for the three days a week I am spending in churches and Bible studies, trying to manipulate God into "saving" John. I need work dresses for some sort of office job that I don't have, and I need date-night dresses for all the dates Bacardi 151 and I are going on.

Somewhere between Tommy Hilfiger and Guess, I realize my deep need for a Christmas dress. Something appropriate to wear to our family's annual Christmas Eve dinner. The perfect dress that says to our families, "John and I are totally solid and more in love than ever, and he hasn't been cheating on me every single minute of every single day since he's met me." Oh, and it has to go with my new $120 pair of sparkly silver Aldo heels.

When I found *the dress*, I just knew.

Tanya, my new best friend and saleslady, has to go to the stock room to see if they carry this amazing silver, silk, strapless dress in a size zero.

They don't. That's OK, though; I'll spend extra money getting the size-two dress tailored down.

Tanya informs me that the dress alone costs $220, and with alterations and tax, it'll be closer to $300.

John will be pissed, I think to myself. And he was, especially when I wore jeans and a sweater to Christmas Eve dinner and never found an occasion to wear that dress.

Orgasm.

I was recalling the memory of the Christmas dress I never wore while having sex with Hot Neighbor a few years after John's suicide. What was happening during these postaffair trauma shopping sprees and what was happening on Hot Neighbor's coffee table both came from the same place inside me: anger or, as we renamed it earlier, murderous rage.

Rage, like Beyoncé, cannot be contained. None of the stages of grief can be, nor should they. Grief will always find a way out of our bodies, and when it does, if you happen to have a vagina, you will be told the anger stage of your grief is unhealthy and unladylike, no matter how you chose to express it. Much like men are told that crying makes them effeminate.

From the time our genitals form in the womb, it seems as if little girls are taught to repress certain things that have been deemed by society as "unfeminine." Anger is one of them.

If we yell, we are crazy.

If we fuck, we are sluts.

If we are on social media, we are attention seeking.

If we shop, we are frivolous and deflecting.

I could write a book twice the length of the Bible about how we are also taught not to use crude language, possess body hair, or raise our voices above a whisper. God forbid we have a natural bodily function that smells or makes sounds…but I digress.

You and you alone determine what things in your life are a *repression* of your grief or an *expression* of it. Are you running *from* your grief and to the outlet mall, or are you running *into* your grief and finally unearthing your rage? Are you using another human to sedate you with orgasms, or are you foregoing orgasms and still leaving that encounter feeling satisfied? Do you look back at your social media rants from last year and feel embarrassed, or do you feel vindicated?

Chapter 20

No

I have been sexually assaulted by four different men. Wait, no—the second one was rape.

With the first guy, I froze and pretended to be asleep.

With the second guy, I froze and I cried, and I bled.

With the third guy, I froze and smiled because I knew I could leave him now.

With the fourth guy, things were different.

I had been widowed for a little more than two years. It was one of those days when nothing took the pain away. It was one of those days when the alcohol just felt like water, and the air around me made me numb and irritable. By 2:00 p.m., I'd had sex with three men. A marine, a guy who had pierced nipples, and one who didn't speak English. None of these encounters resulted in an orgasm. The fourth man I met at a bar. He had a bald head and dangerous eyes, so naturally I went to his house.

I don't know why or exactly when I changed my mind. I remember his head between my legs and a hazy feeling of almost-clarity that came in the form of questions. Do I like this? Am I enjoying this? What do I really want to do right now?

Then a lucid, genuine desire: I want to be at home in my bed, watching *Auntie Mame* on Amazon Prime. I repeated this in my head twice, and that's when everything went from fog to focus.

I told him I was done, and he said he wasn't.

I told him I was feeling sick from the alcohol, and he told me I was just fine.

I sat up, and he forced me back down with his hands.

I tried to pull my underwear up from my ankles, and he ripped them off.

I told him to please stop, and he ignored me.

I screamed for him to stop, and he put three fingers inside me.

At first, I froze. I froze like so many other times in my life, paralyzed by the fact that I had been born with a hole between my legs, and men had been born with power. And then I started to get angry while lying there, staring at the Spackle on his celling. My whole life since John died had been about doing shit I didn't want to do…paperwork, grocery shopping, smiling, driving, feeding myself, getting out of my fucking bed every morning…now all I wanted to do was watch my favorite old movie, and this bald man with the dangerous eyes was keeping me from it?

No.

Just before my knee made contact with his nose, I thought, *Michelle, he could kill you*, and then I thought, *I don't care. I've been dead for years.* When his hands went to his face in surprise, I used my momentum to grab my purse as I rolled off the bed and ran. I could hear him yelling as I ran down the stairs but didn't look back until I got to my car. He was standing there in the frame of his open sliding-glass doors, naked, silent, and waving my panties and sandals at me.

As I drove off, there was disappointment, and then there was shame. I was disappointed that I would never see my panties or sandals again, and I was ashamed that I hadn't kneed him hard enough for his face to bleed.

No one ever told me widowhood was going to be so empowering.

Chapter 21

Depression Takes

The first thing depression took from me was food.

Everyday food experiences assaulted my senses. Hearing a food wrapper made me cringe. Seeing a food commercial gave me a thick feeling in the back of my throat. Touching the kids' lunch boxes made me cry. Smelling the bakery at the grocery store made me vomit, and tasting anything other than unsweetened black tea during the early months of John's first affair revelation was out of the question.

The next thing depression took was the house. My living space became a window into my new depression-saturated brain. Unorganized piles of clutter began to overwhelm each room. My brain and home were filled with foggy, confusing piles of images that could not be understood or categorized. My and John's bedroom was the worst of it.

Depression took my health. I was cold all the time. I'd take hot showers until the water ran cold; dress myself in layer after layer of thermal, cotton, and wool; and then I'd shiver as I drank hot tea. At night, my own chattering teeth would wake me from the semisleep state I had become accustomed to. Even when I was sweating, I had the chills.

The nightmares were vivid and constant: falling, seizing, losing the kids, watching John die while being restrained, losing my teeth, running from a dark figure, and John's friends laughing at me. A violent edge to the sword of trauma, the nightmares would always end with me waking up, drenched in sweat, tears, or blood from gnawing the inside of my mouth raw.

In my waking hours, I obsessively went over every second of my life. What else in my life had all been a lie? What else had I been blinded to? Did God really exist? Was the love my parents had for me genuine, or were they, too, only "playing house" all my life like John had recently confessed to me? Was I actually good at my job, or was my boss talking about me behind my back? Were my children going to suddenly drop dead?

Every second of every day, I was hit over and over again with the realization that everything I had could be taken from me in seconds or that everything I *did* have was not real in the first place.

In one more month, I would weigh ninety-seven pounds, be hooked to a heart monitor, and lose my menstrual periods. Like I said, depression takes.

One of the last things depression took from me was the ability to take care of my children. No, I didn't move out or send them to live with relatives, but I may as well have. I mentally checked out, and my children lost sporadic days, weeks, and months of their mother over the next few years.

Depression didn't just take from me. Depression took from my children.

Of all the insane things you will do in the name of grief, admitting that you are depressed might be the only sane thing that happens. Depression is a completely sane reaction to the death of a spouse, whether it be a physical death, anticipatory death, or death of who you thought he or she was.

I no longer found joy in my children. They were not cute, funny, or interesting; they were not precious to me like they had once been. They were like strange children I was observing at the park. Cute to look at, but I had no instinct to hold, nurture, or even protect them. I was never mean to them, just indifferent, which I believe to be worse. They'd rush enthusiastically to me after school to tell me stories about their little worlds, and all I could think was, "Leave me alone, so I can go back to staring at the wall."

Once sacred moments like the feel of Garrett's fingers when he reached for my hand or the giggle that Belle and I shared when reading bedtime stories were now just reminders to me that I didn't deserve this unconditional love my kids bestowed upon me.

John had made it clear that I was bad. That I was undeserving. That I was worthless. And depression told me to believe him.

Chapter 22

From John's Blog: Thoughts of Pain

February 13, 2014 thirty-nine days before his suicide

Damn this hurts so bad to be away from my family. I can't stop thinking of my wife and what I did and how the fights were not worth loosing my marriage over. The first time we separated after the affair it was nothing like this. I wasn't in love with her anymore and it didn't bother me hardly at all. I know that sounds mean but it was just the state of mind I was in at the time. This time however, I am very much desperately in love with her. This must have been how it was when she found out about the affair for her. It is devastating. I understand why she had to go on anti depressants because I had to do the same. I am on day two of them and day one was better for me. But today it doesn't feel like they are working at all. I just feel like I am in panic mode. I feel like my heart is just going to stop. But that is understandable when you can't even talk to the person you love more than anything.

I thought it would be hard to leave my shop that I worked in every night during the last few years. I mean it was my best friend. When we started fighting I would go out there. If I needed to work on some things I would just go out there. Now I don't have access to it because its on the property with my wife. But I don't miss it at all. I started cleaning it out getting it ready for whoever gets it and I'm just throwing stuff away because none of it really mattered. It was all just stuff in a building. And none of that is more important than my family. I was so stupid for so long and now that I finally realize it it is too late to try and fix because I can't fix the situation. I can't do anything. I can't do anything to try and save my marriage and family. Why? I'm working so hard on myself to become a man but no one will ever know because I don't get any more chances. Damn me for doing that. That is where the pain is coming from I guess. Maybe the pain isn't from missing my family. Maybe the pain is coming from the self inflicted situation.

I don't know, my heads all jumbled and this probably has no structure to it but I just needed to get some thoughts out.

Chapter 23

Widow-Phobia

Widow-phobia is a serious psychiatric condition that occurs in approximately 100 percent of all emotionally ill-equipped, selfish, and insecure men and women. If you have one or more of the signs and symptoms listed below, please call our hotline at 1-800-You-Are-Selfish to be connected with one of our "Healing from Egomania" clinics in your area.

Signs and symptoms include the following:

Finding out your date/friend/family member is widowed and automatically assuming the following:

1. She wants you to marry her right then and there to replace a dead spouse.
2. She wants to move in with you because she is just so pathetic and lonely.
3. She wants you to pay her bills.
4. She's going to expect you to visit her dead partner's grave with her, which would obviously put a damper on your day.
5. She wants you to be Daddy or Mommy to her poor, half-orphaned children.
6. She might…cry.
7. She might, like, cry on her dead spouse's birthday or death-iversary.

8. She might just cry every second of every day.
9. She might have pictures of her dead spouse…everywhere. Even in the…*bedroom*.
10. The spirit of her dead spouse will be watching you when you are having sex with her.
11. Her kids will be needy because obviously they are being raised by an emotionally unstable, lunatic parent.
12. If she didn't have children with her spouse, she will want you to create a child with her right then and there, before the dessert course.

The only known cure for widow-phobia is to attend one of our "Healing from Egomania" clinics, where they will give you the emotional tools you will need to…

get
the
fuck
over
yourself.

You have no idea what you are missing by isolating the widowed. You have no concept of our potential for love, humor, compassion, and openness. You have no idea of the lessons you could be learning from us about what happiness truly is.

And yet, still, even with my own personal revelations of how positively my character has been affected by widowhood, if I could go back to my married bubble, I would. Even with the abuse and adultery that occurred toward the end of my marriage, I would still choose John over this life.

But I can't choose this. He took that choice away from me with his shotgun.

He is gone forever, and so are the dreams I had dreamed for myself and my kids in my twenties. New choices must be made. So I choose to make the best of the life I still have by surrounding myself with fellow widows and those of you nonwidowed out there who have been confident and brave enough to draw me closer with each passing day.

Chapter 24

Grief in the Shower

John had been telling me every day since I had met him a month earlier that we were going to get married, and finally, I agreed to go on a date with him to Calico Ghost Town. He asked me to bring Isabelle, who was just eighteen months old at the time.

It was May in the Mohave Desert and so hot that I dressed Belle in a soaking-wet tank top and shorts to keep her from overheating. The tank top was pink.

We wandered up and down and in and out of the small tourist town that day, unknowingly fabricating the bonds that would one day turn us into a family.

"Wanna meet my grandparents?" he asked me as we loaded the baby into her car seat that evening.

"I'm not dressed for grandparents," I said, motioning to my Daisy Duke shorts and tube top.

Somehow we still ended up in the cozy living room of his kind grandparents, watching Belle color a page of their family scrapbook that I would one day, after his suicide, ache to see again.

On our way back to my apartment, as Belle slept and the setting sun caused John to remove his sunglasses, I suddenly blurted out, "We're going to get married, aren't we?"

He laughed and said, "I've been telling you that for a month!"

A week later, on Memorial Day weekend, he moved in to my apartment, and we began to plan for a fall wedding.

Three years later, on Memorial Day weekend, we moved into our first home. I watched him sweat as he moved boxes, and I nursed our son.

Seven years after that, on Memorial Day weekend, John was gone forever, and I was deep into the home-remodeling phase of my grief, which also happened to overlap with the slut phase of my grief.

I stood in the demolished dining room and called one of the contractors I had hired to remodel my house. We had sex on my and John's bed among the plastic room dividers and sawdust. I silently prayed to him, "Please give me HIV, so I can die."

When that nice man left, I showered, numb. It's weird how depression makes you unable to even feel the sensation of hot water. When I reached for the soap, John's abandoned razor caught my eye as the afternoon sun reflected off its chrome handle in the shower's window ledge. Just hours before he shot a bullet into his torso, he'd shaved his head and face. He wanted to look good in his casket. I had him cremated. As I held the razor, I noticed a single chin hair caught between blades four and five.

Grief is plucking a piece of his hair from blades four and five.

Grief is clutching onto that hair as you fall to your knees in the shower.

Grief is then crawling out of the shower, wrapping yourself in a towel, and saying good-bye to the hair you plucked from blades four and five as it is carried away in a stream of cold water, lost forever through the porthole of his former bathroom sink.

Chapter 25

The Formal Air

John forgot Mother's Day in 2007. We were staying at my parents' house that May while we waited out the lease ending on a lovers' apartment and escrow closing on a family's first home. God, we were young.

I watched John's eyes widen with realization that breezy desert morning as he heard me greet my own mother at the breakfast table with Mother's Day salutations. I was breastfeeding his son. God, I loved playing the martyr.

Off to the corner liquor store John went.

He returned with a fake flower (the ones with the brown, faux-velvet-coated plastic bears attached to the stems), a Three Musketeers candy bar (my favorite), and a look of defeat on his face (oh, such a familiar look this would come to be).

A year later, I spent Mother's Day in a cold, arid hospital room with his toddler son, who was urinating blood. John spent it at home, pretending to have to do a side job to earn money for our son's hospital visit. God, he was comfortable with lies.

I watched John's eyes briefly soften with concern when I brought Garrett home that night as I swaddled his heavy pincushion limbs with a fleece blanket and sang him to sleep. God, our baby was sick.

Off to his friend's house John went.

He returned at 2:00 a.m., smelling of Swisher Sweets (cherry, with a wooden tip), engine exhaust (that smell lived inside his beard and never really went away), and distance (always, he smelled of the formal air that exists between strangers).

"I can't feel anything," he would confess to me later that night as we lay in the darkness. "Just…nothing. I can't explain it." This moment in time is now on the long list of signs I missed, instances in which I failed to look beyond my martyrdom to save my husband from his impending suicide.

Every Mother's Day after this was an extravaganza: breakfasts in bed, flower arrangements, poems, serenades, handmade crafts, living room vacuuming, and dirty-dish scrubbing. He played such a convincing human all those years, as the stench of the formal air that existed between us strangers persisted.

His last words to me in 2014 were screams and moans of agony as he bled out. Finally, he could feel, and so he felt it all.

Weeks after his suicide, on Mother's Day, an order of morning glories from him would arrive.

I threw them in the Dumpster.

Chapter 26

My Chapter Two Does Not Have a Penis

It was the second July since John's suicide and my first July living in San Diego. Lynnette and I were desperate to get away from our five children. We had recently become roommates, and drink-as-we-might to blend our two single-mom families into one, there just wasn't enough alcohol to make this recent cohabitation less noisy and cramped.

So we left the older kids in charge, packed an ice chest, and headed to what has always been our salvation: the beach. This time, though, for added sanity, we went to the nude beach.

Nudity has been such an important part of my grief. Nudity has been such an important part of Lynnette's life. As long as I exist, I will never meet anyone more secure in his or her own skin than Lynnette is. I have learned a lot from her about the kind of power that we as women possess and how to harness this power into the return of the self-confidence my husband had taken from me with his shotgun.

The weather was impossibly perfect—or maybe it's just that my memory of that day was. The humidity was just enough to make the natural waves of my hair bounce but not enough to make them frizz. The sun was bright enough to illuminate Lynnette's tattoos, but the occasional haze of clouds was dark enough to hide the fact that her large tattoos were covering the names of exes.

We spent the first hour or so comparing the genitalia of the nude, middle-aged European men, and then after much laughter, we had to conspire about how to discreetly pee in the ocean. It was decided the best course of action was to wade into the water up to our belly buttons, stay five feet away from each other, and then just let it go while looking out at the horizon and avoiding eye contact with everyone. And so we waded out.

Peeing while naked in the ocean sounds so much easier than it actually is.

Mainly because of the waves and inhibition. One second you're covered by water from your breasts down, and the next the water is at your ankles, and naked strangers will be able to see the yellow trickle running down your legs. From start to finish, it took us both thirty full minutes to intermittently drain our bladders.

When we turned to walk back to the shore, I saw a young couple. He had on Oakley sunglasses, the same kind my husband wore on our wedding day, and she wore an impossibly wide smile, the same kind I had on my wedding day. It was then that I remembered I was a widow.

It was also then that I realized I had forgotten this fact about my life—for the first time in a year and a half—for thirty whole minutes.

Lynnette and I spent the remainder of that day naked and discussing our future. Should we buy a house this year or rent? Did she get my social security number correct when she put me as the beneficiary to her life insurance? Which one of our children is most likely to be gay? Who keeps leaving the dirty dish towels in the sink? Which one of us gets to go on a date this week, and which one of us has to stay home with the kids? Should we attempt to hang our own Christmas lights this year?

Lynnette is my chapter two.

It is widely accepted within the widowed community that a "chapter two," as they call it, is the love you find after your partner's death. I don't know why everyone tends to equate this with romantic love. Sex does not define your chapter two; hope does. Your chapter two is the person, animal, or thing that encourages you to live again and instills you with hope.

Your chapter two is what you are surrounded with in that moment you dare to dream again.

Who or what is your chapter two? Is your chapter two even human? Do you spend your Friday nights planning a road trip with your four-legged friend? If you do, that four-legged friend is your chapter two. Is your chapter two your recent discovery of the peace that washes over you when you perform a monologue on stage for the first time ever? Newfound hobbies, passions, and desires can also be your chapter two.

Think outside the widowed box. Stop lamenting the fact that you may never find romantic love again, and start looking around for the love that is already in your life.

Chapter 27

Dust

I once read that dust is mostly made up of human skin cells. I wondered if John's skin cells were on me then as I watched the brown mist settle on my arms. It had been two weeks since the gunshot that simultaneously oppressed and liberated me. I was sorting through the things my husband had left behind in the garage, the garage we had built years ago for utilitarian purposes that had somehow morphed into a metaphor for John's declining mental health.

This detached, filthy rectangle had slowly become John's retreat when, three years ago, he stopped staying in the house after dinner. Then it became his lover when, two years ago, he stopped sleeping in our bed and preferred the nighttime company of his ever-growing used-car collection and other women. Then it became his asylum when, six months ago, he stopped sleeping altogether and changed the locks on both doors that lead into his fortress.

In his absence, it was not a retreat, a lover, or an asylum. It was a dust-filled, physical oxymoron. Cluttered but hollow, ancient but modern. Laden with sunbeams, but darkened with shadows. The first time I went in there after his suicide, I sat among the things he once touched and knew with certainty that the phrase "time heals" was bullshit.

Time makes things real.

Time removes the merciful veil of shock.

Time is the guilt getting heavier.

Time is discovering yet another question that will never be answered.

Isabelle was just outside the back door of the garage that day, looking down at her feet while balancing on a large metal beam. It was her first time there, too. The long, brown waves cascading from her head made it impossible for me to distinguish the look on her face—not that her face was so easy to read during those early days, but I still wondered what it looked like beneath her hair. She hadn't spoken of her dad since his funeral. She hadn't spoken much at all.

What must this be like for her? I thought. What did I need from my mother when I was eleven years old and mute?

Cake.

Every eleven-year-old girl needs her mother to bring her cake. I grabbed the leftover cake pops from the lunch I'd packed us and asked her to join me. She nodded her head no. So the cake pop and I went to her, out in the desert heat with its unrelenting rays of sun that seem so disrespectful to the cloud that had settled over our lives. She was softly crying.

"Did you remind Daddy of me when he told you he was going to kill himself on the phone?" she said, still focusing on her feet.

It was in that moment that I decided I was ready to date. Yes, two weeks after my husband's suicide, I was ready to date. Not because I wanted to get remarried, not because I was healthy and so full of love that I couldn't wait to share it with someone. No. I decided I was ready to date because *fuck him*.

That afternoon I had the conversation with her, my firstborn, about how nothing anyone said could have talked the gun out of his hand. About how that wasn't even Daddy's voice on the phone when he died because his brain was so very sick. About how his sick brain thought she'd be better off if he was dead. About how his suicide was no one's fault. As I said these things to her, I knew that I didn't completely believe them myself, but I said them anyway.

A few days later, I left the kids in the care of my parents, went out of town, and met with the man who would become the fourth chapter in my memoir, *Boys, Booze, and Bathroom Floors*. And then every weekend after that, I dated a different man. And sometimes the same man. And sometimes four men in a day. I used them, and they used me, and I am a better person today because of it.

Dating gave me an outlet for my rage and respite from the guilt, and it introduced me to my new self. No, I did not meet the next great love of my life out there in the modern social media–infused dating world. No, I did not meet a man who helped piece back together the broken fragments of my once optimistic soul. But I did meet a widowed woman named Michelle who raged until she could finally find the courage to be sad, who withheld the guilt until she was strong enough to absorb it, and who put her own damn soul back together, jaded though it might still be.

Dating can be used for all kinds of purposes, not just an eventual marriage. For me, it has been healing, and I get so much criticism for it, but I'm too busy being wined and dined to care. Not everyone's path to self-discovery and healing after loss is the same, but everyone has one, and people are obligated to their future, healthier selves to find it.

Chapter 28

Fourteen New Year's Resolutions for the Widowed

1. Shave your legs once every six months.
2. Stop caring about people's opinions of your hairy-ass legs.
3. Hire a scientist to invent false eyelashes that stay put after thirty-two straight minutes of crying in the bathroom stall at work or at Target.
4. Use the f-word less.
5. Just kidding. Fuck appropriate language.
6. Find the correct ratio of Benadryl to wine that will help you sleep for more than two consecutive hours a night.
7. Refrain from using your middle finger when someone says, "So you must be feeling better, since it's been a whole two years since your husband died."
8. Just kidding. Flip them off, even if you're in a church.
9. Wear a sign that says, "I'm not divorced, I'm widowed" on all your dates to avoid the awkward "So how long have you been divorced?" question.
10. Develop an unhealthy obsession with a Netflix series; pair it with ice cream or popcorn.
11. Develop a crush on a celebrity. Have his or her face printed on a pillow, and cuddle and talk to it every night. (But not Jared Leto or Channing Tatum because they belong to me.)

12. Wear a black veil with a pink sundress to run errands at least once a week. Everyone thinks you're crazy anyway. You might as well give them reason.
13. Oh, and shower once a week.
14. Make it your mission to find *your* tribe of widows. Some widows grieve with inspirational quotes, comfort foods, and quilts made out of their dead husband's underwear. Some widows grieve with cocktails, rap music, and excessive usage of the phrase, "I hate everything." Both types of widows and all the types in between are brave and scared, strong and weak. All are beautiful in ways that I cannot write. Seek out your tribe if you haven't already. You will feed one another the validation required to begin and continue this life you did not ask for.

Chapter 29

Choices and Cheeseburgers: How We Spent the One-Year Anniversary of His Suicide

I had to make a lot of choices during the first year following John's suicide. Choices I was ill-equipped to make considering the fact that in those early days, my shock-saturated brain kept making me leave the house with two completely different types of sandals on my feet. Decisions such as, sell the house or keep it? Roll John's retirement fund into my Roth IRA or cash it out to pay off his debt? And the routine middle-of-the-night panic attack I affectionately named the "how will I afford medical insurance?" freak-out.

Because life had the audacity to just keep going on, these vital financial decisions had to be pondered simultaneously with the truly significant questions in my new life like, should I stay in bed for the third day in a row, or should I attempt to shower and pretend to be a human today? Should I chug the liter of vodka that's in my freezer, or should I just put the vodka in an IV bag and let it drip into my veins until bedtime? And most pressing of all, what do I do with my dead husband's dirty underwear?

As the one-year anniversary of John's suicide approached, I faced yet another decision. How do I commemorate such a thing? Do I commemorate such a thing? Do I take flowers to his grave? Would my all-consuming rage even allow me to put flowers on his grave, or would I succumb to my hatred and light the cemetery on fire instead? Should I make some sort of baked good? How many carbohydrates would be in said baked good? Should I post a sappy poem on Facebook? What will the kids want to do on this day?

As the weeks drew near, I felt an increasing sense of anxiety. Utopian photos and stories about John had already begun surfacing on social media, and everyone would be expecting to see something similar from me. Only I had nothing like that to share. The man all these people were memorializing was not the man I had come to know during our ten-year relationship. He was so much more complex and dark than the rose-colored photos of him smiling in front of his race car. I guess no one bothered to look past his smile and into the void that was his eyes.

Maybe I should fake it and spend the day in a black veil on his grave after posting pictures of our wedding day to my Facebook wall. Being disingenuous would surely make everyone else feel comfortable.

Thankfully, though, in the last year I'd developed the ability to stop caring about the comfort levels of others in reference to my grieving process. The only thoughts and opinions I cared about now were those of my twelve-year-old daughter and eight-year-old son. So I decided I would do whatever they wanted to do on the anniversary of their father's death. I would be gentle and sensitive to whatever they decided would ease their suffering on this day. If they wanted me in a black veil, I would drape myself in miles of black tulle. If they wanted to lay flowers on his grave, I would buy them ten thousand roses. If they wanted to run a way and hide, I would take them to Jupiter.

Turns out, they wanted cheeseburgers.

Yes, cheeseburgers. It was that simple. When presenting them with the traditional options of a grave-site visit to lay roses or a balloon release on the beach, they were both quiet for several seconds before Garrett asked if we could eat cheeseburgers that day instead, since the other options sounded "boring."

Isabelle took some convincing, although not much, since she loves cheeseburgers almost as much as I love anything drenched in cream cheese frosting. Her main concern was this: cheeseburgers made her happy. Was it OK to be happy on such a day? I eventually convinced her (and myself) that yes, it was. Feeling however you want to feel on whichever day of the year you feel it was always OK.

On the morning of the anniversary, I was surprised to find that I felt nothing. Not like the numb I'm-so-depressed-I-can't-even-taste-ice-cream nothingness I'd become accustomed to. No, this was not a nothingness per se; it was a normal-ness. I took the kids to school, ran errands, and made lunch.

In the afternoon I checked my social media to find exactly what I had expected: photos and stories of a man whom everyone felt they knew. People still expressing shock over the way he had died and countless sappy, overused poems with floral arrangements and beach sunsets in the background. Poems with rhyming words. Poems that made the general population feel comfortable with the way in which they were expressing their grief.

I am not the general population. As a matter of fact, since John's death, I had done nothing the general population had approved of. I drank, I online dated, and I documented every bit of it on social media.

I became enraged the more I scrolled. How dare they? How dare these people point out that John was a hard worker, when he was barely going to work three days a week toward the end! How dare they call him a good father, when he abandoned my babies with the pull of his trigger! How dare they bombard my eyes with pictures of him smiling, when he hadn't smiled at me in three years! He was not a happy person! He was not a nice person! He was not noble!

At least, he wasn't those things to me anymore.

He had become cruel, disconnected, and unpredictable. He didn't sleep. His diet consisted of Little Debbie snack cakes, frozen pizza, and a two-liter bottle of Pepsi every single day for years. He lived in the garage filled with dust and grease from the dozens of car projects he had started but never finished. He lived in the garage with other women who would strip away my self-esteem through their phone calls, online chats, and occasional midnight visits. He lived in the garage with the survival gear he'd accumulated when he had become convinced the end of the world was imminent. Where were the stories and pictures of that?

They were inside of me and the kids—the only ones who had been subjected fully to this side of him. The side of him I chose to leave six weeks before he took his life. The sides people were sharing on social media were fake. They were the masks he'd put on to convince people that he was healthy, and these people did think he was healthy.

My rage subsided at this realization because these people were grieving a healthy version of John. A version I was slowly forced to grieve over the years as I watched his sanity slip from him. I remember this pain. My rage quickly turned to empathy, and my empathy turned into an understanding of why these people had to grieve in this way; remembering him fondly felt natural to them, like cheeseburgers seemed natural to my children. How could I judge these people for grieving in such a way when part of me still feared being judged by them for eating cheeseburgers?

What if no one judged another for how he or she chose to grieve? What kind of world would that be?

That evening, when we all reached the milkshake course of our meal at Ruby's Diner, the mood had gone from normal to downright happy. Silly, even. The three of us were laughing about the chocolate dripping from my son's chin and the noise my daughter's thigh made each time she peeled it from the pleather cushion of our booth.

Not once did we speak of John. He just simply never came up. I never asked myself, "What was I doing a year ago right now?" I was too busy enjoying the presence of my children and the elation of freeing myself from my low-carb lifestyle for the day.

The mood-boosting ability of complex carbohydrates cannot be overstated.

So many other times in the past 365 days had been devoted to the act of mourning. And it is, like love, an action: random Wednesdays when the smell of a stranger's Swisher Sweet cigars sent me into crying convulsions, John's birthday when we reminisced about how much he loved German chocolate cake, Fourth of July when we each pointed out which firework we think Daddy would've liked best, Saturday mornings at 3:00 a.m. when my nightmares were so vivid, they induced an asthma attack.

Yes, so many days and weeks and moments in that first year had been devoted to thoughts and actions about him—missing him, crying for him, regretting not having done enough for him, celebrating him. But on that day, one year after he took his life, we chose to celebrate us: our resilience, our mutual love of greasy cheeseburgers, and our ability to still laugh about the arbitrary things that make up life, like milkshakes on chins and thighs on pleather.

We had made it through the first year intact, and we will make it through so many more. Together. Inseparable. Adhered to one another through our tragedy and triumph like cheese adheres to meat patties.

Chapter 30

My Diary Entries from the Affair Years

November 28, 2011

I am insane. The thought of work makes me want to die. The thought of staying home makes me want to die twice. I hate him. I love him. I trust him. I don't. I want to run away and start over again on a beach. I am ugly and flabby. I look uglier as the slow days pass. I know he did something with Ho2, and I cannot continue until he admits it. I want to hold a gun to his head until he tells me the truth about her, and then I want to pull the trigger. If only I was crazy enough to go through with it. Something has to give.

December 8, 2011

He will never know the ways I loved him. He can't fathom how amazing he was to me. I used to get goose bumps when he walked into a room. Even after six years, my heart would beat fast when he looked at me. He was everything to me. I never felt worthy of him. I always felt like I owed him for being with me and Belle. So I gave him whatever he wanted. Money when we couldn't afford it, project cars when we had no space, sex when I didn't want to, or the freedom to go out with his friends anytime while I watched the kids, even though most nights I was scared and lonely.

I let him off the hook for responsibilities, yard work, family functions, and taking the kids to the doctor, all because I felt like I owed him and all because I wanted to keep him happy so that he wouldn't cheat or leave. The few times I did ask for help with the kids or if we could save the money instead of spend it, I'd feel guilty. Guilty for what? For expecting him to be a man? He chose this life, and he only wants the good parts of it. He wants the look of a family but the life of a bachelor. I always feared one day he'd realize what he gave up by becoming a husband and father at such a young age and then resent me for the rest of his life. That time is here. I loved him so much over the years. How could he still be lonely? I thought I loved him enough for the both of us.

January 13, 2012
Nothing takes the pain away. Even when I'm feeling happy, I know it's only temporary. Shopping, friends, manicures, Rollerblading—it never takes the pain completely away. I wake up each morning, and my mind runs a slide show of the past eight years and mostly the past six months. I used to love mornings. Moving slowly, sipping tea, reading my Bible, and looking at the sunrise. Now I have to rush, hurry up, and fill my day with something, or my mind will fill with despair. When will there be joy again? Will there ever be a day or an hour when I don't think of the girls he cheated with?

March 13, 2012
I woke up on a gurney in the hospital today. I went into the doctors for a checkup to see how my body is responding to the antidepressants, and the last thing I remember was being in the waiting room. They kept me all day for observation and labs. They couldn't figure out why my blood pressure was so low. My blood work showed deficiencies in several vitamins, which explained my hair loss and loose teeth. When the doctor asked if I was having any other symptoms, I cried uncontrollably and told him my husband doesn't love me and never did and that he had cheated on me for years. What a psycho I am. He wrote things in his notebook. The hospital

kept trying to get ahold of John, but he never answered his phone. My mom sat with me the rest of the day.

December 20, 2013
Another year of my life gone, wasted on him. I'm exhausted all the time. If he were dead, I'd be free—mostly, anyway. Freedom is an illusion. I'd love to one day say, "I'm going to the store" and not get the third degree. I'd love to pick out my own clothes instead of coming out of the shower every day to see that he's laid out an "appropriate outfit" I'm forced to wear, an outfit that hides anything on my body that I like. I'd love to go one day—just one day—without thinking about his affairs. I'd love to think for myself and about myself. I'd love to leave this town and start over fresh. I hate Christmas; it's so depressing, so anticlimactic. The kids are growing up so fast, and I'm such an empty shell that I'm missing it.

December 25, 2013
It took me two minutes to fall in love with him and two years to fall out. I really think this is it. I really think it's over. The pros and cons have been measured. I am ready. I wish I didn't know how ugly these things could get, how vicious people become, or how many people I could lose. Still, even with the fear, the thought of staying seems worse. Can I really do this? Be single again? Take my kids back and forth between two homes? Go through a war…the endless battles for control? The fears? Will my babies be better for it or worse?

December 26, 2013
I really thought it'd be forever. I never saw it getting here. I don't love him. I want out. I cheer myself up with thoughts of alimony, double the closet space, and freedom. It's so against my nature to hurt someone's feelings. I wish he were mean all the time. I wish I hadn't come home to a dozen red roses and a spotless house. I wish these things he did were actually for me and not for his ego. I wish for a lot of things. My babies, my loves…I have failed them. It's too late now. I should've left two years ago. Did I

misinterpret the signs? Did God really want me to stay? If so, why do I feel so strongly that I should leave? Why now? Is this what I get for my crimes? The confusion cannot be understated.

December 29, 2013

I want out. I told him I didn't love him and want a divorce, and he blamed it on my period and depression. God forbid he ever takes responsibility for anything.

Chapter 31

Why Don't You and Jesus Pick Up the Dog Shit?

I am alone. Even before he was dead, I was alone. Every holiday, every birthday, every day of the week, every night in my bed, it's just me.

I am done with people serving me the bullshit of, "You're not really alone. You have me and your family!" or "Jesus is with you right now." OK, fine! Why don't you and Jesus pick up the dog shit and help me shop for the kids' Easter baskets?

Go ahead and tell me I'm *not* alone. I dare you.

The edge of loneliness is being softened by men. The hunt, the chase, and the eventual victory have been like a warm bath and a cocktail, but with occasional orgasms. The only downfall is that I am begrudgingly finding empathy for John's sex addiction. Grrrrrrr.

My therapist says I show signs of a dopamine deficiency and am using men to medicate myself. He wants me back on the antidepressants.

"So what?" I say. "Some people use food to comfort themselves; other people use sex."

"Agreed, but food can't give you STDs and unwanted pregnancies," he challenges.

"I'd rather have an STD than be fat," I shoot back, without skipping a beat.

He knows I panic when my weight balloons to anything over 120, which I know is ridiculous because for my age and height, I'd be perfectly thin if I weighed 135 pounds.

His forehead wrinkle is prominent, meaning he is genuinely concerned.

"I don't eat when I'm high on men," I tell him. Then I share with him the story of when I was French kissed for the first time by a boy who wasn't my boyfriend.

I was twelve, and he was thirteen. We had been looking at each other across the lunchroom for months when one day he grabbed my hand, took me behind the ball court, and kissed me. We never spoke or looked at each other again. I couldn't eat for seven days, and my mom made me go to the school counselor, who talked to me about anorexia.

But I wasn't anorexic—I was high. Every waking moment was spent fantasizing about the kiss. The fantasies *were* my food.

My current weight is 110, courtesy of Chad, Ky, Tim, James, Matthew, and Lenny. Jeremy dumped me a week after John's suicide because he felt it would be better for me to grieve without being distracted by him. Poor idiot thought he was the only guy I was talking to. He wants to attempt a relationship in six months when I'm "healthier." Fuck him; I had him replaced two hours later with a quick Facebook message to Tim. When I see Jeremy at church, I want to punch him in the face.

I spent this past weekend with Chad in LA again. While I was nearing my second orgasm (yes, he's that good), my phone kept going off, and I stopped to check it just in case it was the kids. It wasn't. It was Ky, Tim, and James, all wanting *me*.

I'm sure Chad knows I'm seeing other men, but he doesn't ask, nor does he seem to care. I know he doesn't really like me, just what my body can do for him, and for the time being I don't mind being used by him, because I am using him as well—for meals, for companionship, for an escape. Isn't that all romantic relationships are, anyway? Two people getting what they need from each other before ultimately walking away? Chad owes me. All the men owe me. They will pay for John's cruelty. They will give me back the self-esteem he took…or did I give the self-esteem to him freely?

Chapter 32

Hairapist versus a Therapist

Your therapist will listen to you ramble and will jot notes down on a yellow legal pad. Your hairapist will listen to you ramble and then talk shit with you about all the people you hate.

Your therapist will nod empathetically. Your hairapist will say, "That asshole did *whaaaat*?"

Your therapist will hand you tissues when you cry. Your hairapist will hand you wine and a magazine with all the latest hair trends.

Your therapist will encourage you to set boundaries and be a better version of yourself. Your hairapist will accept all the versions of yourself and style each one of your multiple personalities.

Your therapist will say, "So how are you doing?" Your hairapist will say, "What the hell is going on? This is from stress!" as she steps back, holding a fistful of your hair.

Your therapist will hand you a bill. Your hairapist will hold a fund raiser days after your husband dies, and you will find yourself sitting in the parking lot of her salon, holding a large envelope with enough cash in it for you and your children to live off for five months. You will never really find the words to thank her, so you will put this chapter in your book for her to read instead.

Chapter 33

Lived

One of John's last Augusts on earth, he forgot my birthday, but I still got flowers. I would find out a few months later that Ho2 saw my birthday reminder on her Facebook and sent me flowers with his name on it to save his ass.

A week after my birthday, he lied and told me that his debit card didn't work that day and that she, our mutual friend, paid for the flowers with her card, so now we owed her sixty dollars. We didn't have sixty dollars because two weeks prior to my birthday, John had bought a 2006 Cadillac without asking me.

Hello, manic episode.

My mom had given me a hundred dollars for my birthday, and I gave sixty of it to my husband's girlfriend for the flowers, under the belief that John would pay me back on payday. Of course he never did.

This is the only one of my birthdays with him that I can remember. Ten fucking birthdays spent with my husband, and this is all I have in my memory bank. I'm sure there were good ones, but my hatred won't let me recall any of them.

A lot of people think that suicide is a sudden death. It. Is. Not. My husband's death took place in front of my eyes for three years before the gunshot, and that birthday (I think it was my twenty-ninth) is evidence of it.

When I attended Camp Widow San Diego for the first time, there was a fake river with real rocks. Each camper had to write a word on a rock and place it in the river for an unknown someone who needed it, while they picked up a rock that had a word on it that they needed.

Corny? Yes. But after the gallon of vodka I'd ingested that night, I knew my mission in life was to find *the* rock. The rock that would explain it all. The rock that would comfort me. The rock that would make my life make sense again. The rock that would explain to me why in the hell I was even at a place called Camp Widow. Yes, this rock would be my salvation.

You know you have had a lot of vodka when you are looking for comfort in a rock.

As I combed the fake beaches of the fake river, there were typical words like "love," "laughter," "peace," and "joy." I skipped all of those, knowing not to even bother with affirmations that are too far out of reach for someone like me.

Then, at the end of the fake river, I saw a rock that said, "LIVED" in all capital letters, followed by a happy face. Vodka and I felt drawn to it, but we both really hated that happy face, so we continued looking for another rock that had the same word minus the happy face.

We couldn't find one. There was "live," and "life," but no past-tense "lived." We snatched up the "lived" rock and glared at the happy face before putting it into my black, fringed clutch.

Why "LIVED"? Because before John died, he had lived. Before John died, I had lived. There was love, and there was laughter, and there was joy, and there was peace. I don't think about this most days. I prefer to focus on his slow, painful death and all the pain he inflicted on me while actively dying. I prefer to focus on his hatred as well as my own.

Hatred makes the despair of my grief more tolerable, and today, like most days, I choose the hate. But knowing that for a moment vodka and I were drawn to the word "LIVED" means that one day we might also be drawn to the love, and to the laughter, and to the joy, and to the peace that once was and that could be again.

Chapter 34

Four Widow-Approved Ways to Avoid the Holi-daze

I hate Christmas. There, I said it. I wasn't always this way, of course, but something about life in post-infidelity and post-spousal-suicide land just brings out the Grinch in me. Call me crazy (like my therapist did that first year, when he wrote a note to my doctor, pleading with her to put me on Effexor). This year, I am approaching my sixth round of holidays since my Martha Stewart self was metaphorically murdered in the fall of 2011 by the discovery of John's affairs, and I want to share with you all how I have managed to survive the previous holidays using my favorite of all the coping methods: complete and total avoidance.

Before you judge me for being a bad mother for letting my grief usurp my kids' holiday experience, know this, my self-righteous readers: even in the lowest moments of my holiday grief, I still gave my kids the obligatory holiday experience they desired. I just simply wasn't emotionally present for any of it.

Sidenote: I don't think children give a fuck about their parents' emotional presence when Xboxes, iPhones, and sugar cookies are involved.

I still cooked, shopped, wrapped, semidecorated (Oh no! We must've lost the seventeenth box of Christmas crap when we moved, and now we will have to survive with only boxes one through sixteen), and read the stories. I watched the movies and sat through church and school plays (with sunglasses on to hide my tears). It just happened to be that I did not have the holiday spirit dwelling within me when I performed these tasks.

And they were *tasks*.

I used to think my lack of holiday cheer was yet another thing that John and his whores took from me. Now I realize that I willingly gave up my holiday spirit to begin the lifelong grief war I was forced into fighting. I could've used the holidays to avoid my grief, but instead I used my grief to avoid the holidays. Looking back now, I realize how very brave this was.

So here you go, the four widow-approved methods to avoid the holiday season and focus on your grief (I promise these don't involve self-help books, therapy sessions, or Bible verses):

1. Replace your Advent calendar with high-heeled boots.

As I mentioned in a previous chapter, during the fall of 2011, I shopped the hell out of my grief. This in turn left me with a vast collection of high-heeled boots. I literally wore a different pair of boots every single day in December of 2011. The staff ornament exchange at work was no longer a depressing display of holiday decorations; it became "camel-colored wedge, calf-high-boot day." Garrett's kindergarten class's hour-long sing-a-thon was not an evening of being surrounded by happily married parents cuddled together on cafeteria benches; it became the night I got to show off my black, suede, thigh-high, five-inch-tall, sex-kitten boots. (It should be noted that my ass looked amazing in the leggings I paired with this.)

Every new day in December became an opportunity for me to concentrate on myself (the season for giving, be damned!) and identify what made me happy…in between six hour–long stints of stalking the other women, vomiting, and then crying until my back was too sore to walk. Nonetheless, the point is, doing something nice for yourself is a great distraction from the holiday season and a great way to begin the healing process, even when you are in so much pain, you can't possibly notice you are healing until years later.

My advice to you is this: make a grief Advent calendar, and write on it one thing each day you will do for yourself. Note a manicure, a day you will purposely call in sick to work to have a *Grey's Anatomy* marathon, or a meeting with a friend (preferably one whose life sucks worse than yours) for cocktails.

2. Go to the (fake) Bahamas…and drink a lot of alcohol while you are there.

During the holiday season of 2012, it was not uncommon for my cheating husband to come home from work to find me in my bathing suit, listening to Bob Marley while drinking margaritas with the thermostat set to 85. "Something about the cold weather feels like death!" I would say to him. "I need to be alive! Don't you just want to be alive? Don't you want to be free?" He would ask where dinner was and wonder aloud how many milligrams of Cymbalta I was currently on.

I'm pretty sure 2012 was my kids' favorite of all my holiday avoidance strategies, not only because they found the contrast of the Christmas decorations and me in a bathing suit to be hilarious, but also because Margarita Mommy didn't give a shit if they finished their homework or not (so much for me avoiding your judgment about what a bad mother I am).

Part of the grieving process is giving up control. I would venture to say that on some level, the entire grieving process is about letting go of control of the idea that you even had control to begin with. Grieving is realizing that shitty things happen to wonderful people. It is also realizing that there is no such thing as wonderful people. It is accepting that we are all broken, and then it is learning to find joy in spite of this awful realization about humanity. Celebrate this epiphany. Celebrate it in bathing suits and ball gowns, in kitchens and driveways.

My advice to you is this: go somewhere that makes you feel free, and if you can't afford it, bring the freedom to you. Pair this activity with an appropriate frosty drink, summer-themed music, and, of course, a bathing suit that makes you feel powerful.

3. Throw a fit.

My entire holiday season of 2013 was spent in a series of heated battles within the marital war I'd been waging since 2011. In November of 2013, I'd finally weaned off all of my antidepressants, pulled my head out of my ass, looked around, and said, "Why the fuck am I OK living with a controlling, mentally abusive adulterer who refuses to get help? Why am I on meds and in counseling when I've done nothing wrong? Why is he telling me what I can and cannot wear when his computer is filled with photo diaries of his infidelity?"

Fuck holiday cheer! That season, I dug my heels into the ground, stood up for myself, acknowledged my anger, and gave myself permission to express it in as ghetto of a way as possible. Dammit, I made every single person around me uncomfortable that year in the name of expressing my grief.

> HOLIDAY PARTYGOER: Where's John at today? Working late?
> ME: No, he's throwing things in the garage because I'm wearing a V-neck sweater.
> HOLIDAY PARTYGOER: So what did you get the hubsters for Christmas?
> ME: The gift of not posting pictures of him and his whores on Facebook. It's so nice of me not to do this considering how they are all married whores, and their husbands own guns.

A few months later, John would be dead. I often wonder if I'd have behaved differently that holiday season had I known this. I wonder if I had had the knowledge that hypersexuality, paranoia, and irritability can be symptoms of an array of mental illnesses if I would have still been so angry. Possibly not.

Don't put on the happy holiday show if you aren't happy. Speak your mind, feel the feels, and make people uncomfortable with your rage or your sorrow. Those who matter will love you through this, and they will probably make you a strong drink.

4. Sleep with everyone in town so that you are forced to move.

The first part is optional, but I can tell you from experience that promiscuity in a small town is a great relocation motivator as you've probably read in my memoir, *Boys, Booze, and Bathroom Floors*. As the first holiday season after John's suicide approached in 2014, my level of anxiety increased. I felt like a caged, slutty animal and had an unshakable instinct to take my kids to a remote island.

Remote-island living turned out to be devoid of In-N-Out Burger franchises, so I decided to go with the next best choice: my pups and I relocated to San Diego. I signed a lease four days before Thanksgiving, and on December 18, the moving truck followed us to our new lives. With all the decluttering, cardboard-box hoarding, packing, and watching hot men load moving trucks, I didn't have the time or energy to hate all the couples in matching flannel on social media, let alone plan a holiday.

Ultimately, the kids spent Christmas Eve and Christmas Day with their grandparents while I drove around crying and drinking Starbucks. This might sound a bit depressing, but to me, spending only two days out of my first holiday crying like a—well, like a widow on her first holiday season—was a victory.

I could've waited until after the holiday season to move. I could've done all the traditional holiday things I did when John was alive, but you know what? Fuck tradition. Tradition made me feel like I was still enslaved to his sick brain. Moving made me take an active role in my new life. It forced me to make a choice about the kind of life I wanted to live and the place where I wanted to live it. Moving instead of cooking his fucking

Christmas breakfast that year empowered me, and I was judged mercilessly for it.

My advice to you is this: move, or don't. Really think about what you want to do for the holidays and not what you are expected to do. And for the love of Beyoncé, add alcohol to your Starbucks latte.

Chapter 35

The Nerve

I have Ho1's schedule memorized (and possibly her license plate, social security number, and the names and phone numbers of no less than ten of her blood relatives, but I will deny this in court should I accidentally get arrested). Months of sleepless nights paired with the energy from my anxiety attacks gives me time to stalk her properly. I don't know why I never focus much energy on the other women John has been with. Maybe it was denial telling me this Ho1 was the only one, and the others should be dismissed because John had been the most in love with her. Maybe it's because I had to see her over and over again in my dreams each night, with her perfect skin and six-pack abs. Or maybe, just maybe, it was because John was heartbroken over finding out that she was fucking one of his coworkers just a few weeks after I made him break up with her.

Have I mentioned how classy she is?

John still loving her after all this time is just another reminder that he does not love me. That he never did. That's OK, though; I know just how to solve this problem: I will go to the tanning salon.

Have I mentioned how crazy I am?

I will go every day. Some days I will tan, and some days I will sit there and chat with the owner until Ho1 shows up, because I know she will show up when she is done with her yoga class.

Today, I see her car pull into the parking lot from the corner of my eye and purposely begin a discussion with everyone in the waiting area about what she did with my husband. I live for this kind of shit. When she walks in, she is welcomed by the knowing stares and awkward midsentence voice trail-off that people have to do when the target of their gossip walks into a room.

She looks so different than she does on her social media profiles. She's always been fifteen years older than me, but today she looks it. Even with her makeup on, her wrinkles are prominent. Her posture is slouched, and her hair…the best part…her hair is slightly unkempt. Still, her designer gym clothes all match. Bitch.

"Hi! How are you today?" I say to Ho1, smiling a bit too widely.

"Good, thanks," she says, with her head down and her voice shaky. Everyone is uncomfortable except me.

Her tanning session is fifteen minutes long. Thirty-two minutes later, she's still in the little room. I try to take pleasure in this, but after minute thirty-five, I have a nagging sense of sympathy for her—until I remind myself that she had the nerve to befriend my unsuspecting mother on Facebook last month.

When Ho1 is coaxed out of the room by the owner insisting there's another client in need of the room, she does the walk of shame in front of me and everyone else down the mirror-lined hallway and out the door to her black BMW.

"Have a great day!" I yell to her. I know I will.

Chapter 36:

Things I Wrote on my Facebook for Our Wedding Anniversary

October 8, 2017

My last three wedding anniversaries without him, I have written lengthy posts that attempt to articulate the complexities of what I feel on October 8. This year, it is simple.

I am sad.

October 8, 2016

Dear John,

Happy anniversary, except it's not happy. You get to be dead, and I get to be here. I'm jealous of that. I'm too tired to be angry at you this year. Too tired to write another lengthy letter to you articulating all the ways in which your suicide killed me. I tried to make this time of year mean something different. I published a book, thinking, *Now this time of year will be the anniversary of me becoming an author.* And it is—but it is also the anniversary of hope and optimism and naïveté and a reminder that I no longer have these traits as parts of my personality. Will this day ever be anything

other than this? Will it ever just be October eighth? I miss you. I miss who I was. I miss who our children were supposed to be.
Fuck you!
Michelle

October 8, 2015
Dear John,
Happy ten-year anniversary. I hate that you gave me the life I always wanted and then took it away from me. I hate that the word "suicide" is a part of my children's vocabulary. I hate that the scent of your skin is no longer on the jacket I bought you on our honeymoon, the jacket I am wearing now as I write this. Please come back and tell me this was all a bad dream.

Dear Michelle "Fan Club,"
Thank you in advance for your private messages today on how to "get over" John's death as you continue to judge and criticize my angry, humorous, and very public social media–infused grieving process. Thank you to those who take it one step further by continuing to blame and socially shun me for John's suicide in addition to the criticizing and judging. Your complete lack of humanity continues to be used to my advantage as I gain more love, compassion, and empathy for others who have survived similar and harsher injustices in life than I.

Dear "Actual" Michelle Fan Club,
Your love continues to outweigh the hate, of which there is an infinite amount. It seems so trite to simply say, "I love you," but I do. Let's eat cake today! If you don't live near me, send me pics of you stuffing your face…alcohol-drinking pics are also acceptable and highly encouraged. But be smart about it; don't drink and Tinder, everyone!
With sincerity,
Michelle Miller

October 8, 2014
Dear John,
The vomiting started this morning at 7:00 a.m. The only thing that took the churning in my stomach away was the sound of Dave Grohl singing, "Best of You," so I put him on repeat. I left work early, lay on your grave, and cried myself to sleep. When I woke up with the hot sun searing down on me, I asked myself, *What do I do now?*

Listen to our wedding song while wearing my dress? Drink a bottle of vodka? Throw myself a pity party? I wish I had these luxuries, but I don't. I don't get to fall apart for more than a few hours.

I have to go to work. I have bills to pay.

I have to go to the gym. I have depression to battle.

I have to go to Bible study. I have a faith that is crumbling.

I have to return the messages on my phone. I have friendships that need to be nurtured.

I have to put a smile on my face. I have children who are watching.

A friend advised me to look at something that makes me feel like a badass today, so I chose to look at our wedding picture. It used to overwhelm me with despair, guilt, and rage. But today all I felt was pride. Pride in myself. I am a badass.

I was a good wife. Not perfect, but amazing. Every day I lived my vows. I was devoted and meticulously faithful. I stayed when others would have left.

So tomorrow and all the days after, as I continue to live in this fishbowl, I will remember this feeling of pride. Even with the stares and the whispers, the dirty looks, the pointing fingers, the judgments, and the rumors that I have been forced to live with, I know I have accomplished what I set out to do nine years ago. I loved you well.
With sincerity,
Michelle

Chapter 37

From John's Blog: Feeling Word of the Day

March 5th, 2014 eighteen days before his suicide
I feel like 24601

Chapter 38

Thirteen Ways That Widows Are like Toddlers

1. We can't be trusted to dress ourselves.

Garrett once bit me because I would not let him wear flip-flops during a hailstorm. I regret glaring at him behind his back as I dropped him off at Sunday school that day, because I get it now. I get what it is like to have your brain so clouded and busy that appropriate apparel rules become too complicated to adhere to.

After John's suicide, I often found myself looking down at my feet in the grocery store, amazed that I had been walking around all day with two different shoes on.

Then there was the time I finally did my laundry (after only two and a half weeks of letting it rot in my closet), only to realize that I had not come across one pair of underwear. I checked my underwear drawer to find every piece of underwear I owned still unmoved from the weeks before. Yes, I had not worn underwear for two weeks.

Which brings me to my next point.

2. We are often naked.

As toddlers, my children loved to be naked. This would have been fine and healthy behavior had it not always been in public. I don't know if they were some sort of exhibitionists or just suffering from hot flashes, but it seemed like every time I looked away from them in public, I would turn around to find them stripping and streaking.

But for me, the widow nudity had nothing to do with hot flashes or exhibitionism. It had to do with the grief sex I was having and the return of my self-confidence as I spent a few hours naked on a beach. And twice in a car. And a few times in other locations that I am sure will surface on the news via Google Earth or a surveillance video one day. (Hi, Mom and Dad!)

Who knew that nudity would be a part of my grief process?

3. We have nightmares.

And they are fucking scary.

4. We are finicky eaters.

News flash: toddlers don't like vegetables. Shocking, yes I know. My son, though, ate dirt, lint, and whatever else he found on the floor with gusto. So one day I just started dropping green beans all over the floor in our house, and lo and behold, I had a toddler who ate vegetables. Oddly enough, when I tried this with Goldfish crackers, he said, "Ewww, Mommy. Fishy dirty," and refused to eat them.

Much like the eating habits of my son (and my daughter, who lived on peanut-butter-and-jelly sandwiches for two years), my eating habits became strange and unpredictable after John's death. After his suicide, I didn't eat for a week. Then the next week, and for a month straight, every night I ate a bowl of peanut butter laced with half a bag of chocolate chips and washed it down with vodka. Six months after his death, I went through a phase in which I only ate organic beef patties and two avocados a day.

Which leads me to the next one…

5. We have unpredictable bowels.

I used to play a game in my head each morning when my kids were toddlers. It was called, "Will their poop be running down their legs and spilling out of their diapers today, or will they be sitting on their potty chairs, making the same face I make when I think about my exes for hours on end?" I hated this game almost as much as I hated Candy Land.

It's like that with widowhood, too—only I was too embarrassed to purchase adult diapers, so I just ruined underwear…unless it happened to be during the aforementioned two-week stint I went without underwear.

6. We have no concept of social norms.

We will say and do weird shit that will make everyone around us uncomfortable. And then we will laugh about it.

7. We throw fits.

In public. And we don't give a damn about who is watching. My son once threw a fit at the bank because they had a Christmas tree up that had a star at the top and not an angel. I whisper-yelled at him through gritted teeth, "*You get your little bottom up right now! People are staring at you!*" He then looked at me as if *I* were the crazy one and proceeded to throw an even louder fit.

I never understood this until a year into widowhood when I found myself yelling at a woman, "Fuck you, you stupid-ass bitch and your ugly-ass car!" while in the pickup line at my kids' elementary school. In front of a row of kindergartners.

I am no longer allowed in the west-side pickup line, but I still, to this day, maintain my innocence.

8. We just want to be held.

Seriously, someone pick me up and rock me.

9. We are entitled.

Both of my kids as toddlers thought that just by being born, they deserved unlimited amounts of TV and assorted sugary pastries. Oh, and they also wanted my complete and total undivided attention and my soul. I remember having a talk with both of them once in the car, trying to explain to them that other people in the world had it worse than them, and they should learn to start being happy that they lived such a charmed life.

My daughter then asked me for a cookie.

Neither of them could conceive of a life in which they weren't having all of their needs met all of the time.

Fast forward to "the widow card." It exists, and it got me out of chores, traffic tickets, and work in addition to a lot of free drinks, meals, and spa treatments that first year in 2014. Then, sometime around 2015, people became less sympathetic to my widowhood. Apparently I had graduated to veteran widow status after the first year had passed, and I no longer was entitled to free shit. Or so they thought.

I am almost three years in to this shit storm, and I can tell you that I absolutely still need free goodies, a lot of understanding, and tons of cocktails every single day for the rest of my life. I pull the widow card out frequently, and I have no shame about it.

10. We need naps.

Like three a day. Minimum.

11. We don't know the days of the week or months of the year.

Even when we sing that damn "Days of the Week" song, we still have no clue what day of the week it is. Widow brain is a thing, people! I wrote a check two weeks ago with the year 2015 on it, and a few months ago I sat at my kids' school for two hours before pickup time because I was convinced that it was early-out Wednesday. Turns out, it was actually Thursday.

My daughter once asked me if Friday was purple. Why, yes. It does appear to be purple now that I am a widow.

My son once insisted that Novebruary was a month, and it needed to involve cake. Sounds good to me, son!

12. Our living spaces are huge messes.

And no, thank you, we will not be cleaning it up, and we will throw things at you if you suggest that we do.

13. We respond well to positive reinforcement.

I once posted to my Facebook how proud I was of myself for showering *and* shaving my legs. I had an overwhelming amount of widows and widow supporters post gold star emojis in the comments. I felt all warm and fuzzy inside, much like I think my kids felt as toddlers when I would put stickers on their little sticker charts to reward them for not sending me to the insane asylum that day.

Widowhood sucks. Widows I talk to express their profound discouragement within the life they exist in. They worry that they are not grieving the "right" way. They worry that they are grieving too much. Crying too hard. Not crying enough. They judge themselves for the six-month-old pile of laundry. They get judged by others for their inability to just "get over it." I want to tell you all that you are doing just fine. Yes, you sitting there reading this with your hairy armpits, ratted hair, and week-old leggings…you are *winning*. You decided to read a chapter with a funny title in search of laughter. Do you even understand how heroic it is to seek out laughter after what you've been through?

Chapter 39

Zombie

In 2013 John truly believed we were on the verge of an actual zombie apocalypse. When I am drunk, I laugh until I cry about this. The hype surrounding *The Walking Dead* and my husband's deteriorating mental state made for some interesting conversations with him in the final years of his life.

"What exactly do you think zombies are?" he hissed at me one night when I attempted to reassure him that zombies were not going to come after us in the middle of the night.

"They're like human bodies without souls that walk around eating brains in horror movies," I said casually, trying to diffuse the situation.

"No. Zombies are normal humans that got injected with toxins from the government, and their brains got eaten alive, and they are so sick from their brains that they try to eat other people. Michelle, this is something that could really happen. It's not just in TV shows!"

The irony of my brain-sick husband trying to educate me on a species of humans with brain sickness did not occur to me until I sat down to write this. Ugh. I'm so over epiphanies. I used to think John's obsession with zombie culture was in part a response to his longing for Ho1. They used to have *Walking Dead* marathons while Yours Truly was blissfully teaching Sunday school in the land of obliviousness. Why had they both chosen to bond over zombies, though? Why had I never been drawn to zombie culture? I want to be a bitch right now and point out the fact that John and Ho1 were both brainless zombies who had checked out of their marriages, but I have too many friends who are also fans of zombie culture and do not happen to be brainless. I also want to be a smug bitch and point out that I am not drawn to zombie culture because I am deep and artistic and all emotionally evolved n' shit…but just the fact that I ended that last part with the phrase "n' shit" disproves this theory altogether.

So what am I getting at with all this zombie reflection? That we are fascinated by and fearful of our weaknesses. John was born with a weak brain. He knew this on some level. He had expressed to me on multiple occasions about his lifelong confusion with emotions and human connection. As a child, when his grandmother died, he confessed to me that he had no feelings about the death. The very next day he found a dead bird in his front yard and cried for hours. "Was that maybe a delayed reaction to the loss of your grandma?" I had asked him.

"No. I really didn't feel sad about her or sad for my mom. I think I cried because I felt bad that I couldn't cry…Like, I knew I was supposed to be sad, but I wasn't, and that made me feel like a monster or something." From then on, to avoid being seen as a monster, John would force himself to react and behave in a way that he believed was appropriate based on his observations of other people.

In adulthood, feigning a genuine connection to me—an empath who is overly emotional and turns the people in her life into living, breathing life-support machines—became too taxing for him, and so naturally he sought respite in the company of others like him who were devoid of emotions and therefore made him feel like less of what he feared becoming: an un-empathetic monster. A zombie.

After his affair with Ho1 came to light, John would spend the next year and a half building a "zombie-rig" from an old Suburban in our garage while stockpiling survival gear and mapping out places in the desert we would be living once the zombie apocalypse happened—and the Zombie apocalypse did happen, just not in the way he'd imagined it.

I would spend the next year and a half building a fortress of denial around myself. *He was just really into* The Walking Dead, I would tell myself. *End-of-the-world prepping is just a trend right now*, I would say as I flipped through TV stations, watching reality shows on the subject.

After his suicide, I would spend hours and hours going through stacks of yellow legal pads with my mouth hanging open and gasps unwillingly surfacing from my throat. I had no idea how thoroughly he had planned for the zombie apocalypse. It took me years to tell anyone about this. I didn't need to admit to yet another sign that I missed.

John's last Father's Day on earth was in 2013. I asked him what he wanted, and he gave me a list of survival gear. I asked if I could just make him his favorite dinner instead. He rolled his eyes at me. And so, I bought $200 worth of survival gear, put it in a large box with tissue paper, and had the kids help me wrap it—all the while trying to convince myself (and the kids) that we were buying all this so that we could start taking camping trips.

I could tell instantly that he disapproved of the survival gear on Father's Day morning. It wasn't the right size, or brand, or color, or whatever. Nothing in John's life was ever the right size, or brand, or color, or whatever. Nothing was ever enough. Nothing was ever good. Still, he feigned gratitude and politely smiled and thanked the kids and me, while I politely accepted and pretended I gave those gifts to him from my heart.

Insincerity: the foundation of our marriage.

Insincerity: the twin sister of denial.

Where John had faked emotions, I had faked ignorance. Continuing my life like this after his death, and perpetuating this cycle in my children, dishonors us both.

So what have I done on Father's Day with the kids since their father's death? I have been asked this question a lot on social media in the weeks leading up to this holiday. For all of the postmortem holidays, I have decided only sincerity will do for the kids and me. The only obligation we now have in this new life is to be honest with what we are feeling and decide for ourselves what we want to do with those feelings, especially within the context of holidays.

So two weeks before a holiday or milestone, I will very casually say, "_____ is coming up in a few weeks. Let me know if you guys would like to do anything for that. We can do whatever you want as long as it costs less than a billion dollars."

Then I remind them a few days before.

Then the morning of, I acknowledge it and say, "Let's go do _____, unless you're just not feelin' it today. Then we can make other plans or do nothing at all." So far, this has worked for our family.

On Father's Day in 2014, I woke up to a vase of flowers that the kids had picked from our garden. *For me.* We climbed a hill and spread John's ashes.

In 2015, we went to his grave and took pictures.

In 2016, we did nothing because they sincerely didn't want to.

In 2017, they wanted to stay with my parents and have a normal day. I wanted to surround myself with widows, Tito's vodka, deep-fried tofu, and music. And so we each did what we wanted to do. My mother sent me pictures of the kids swimming and lounging, and I found myself, at 11:00 p.m., looking around a very crowded table at a very stuffy bar with a group of widows I had, up until that moment, only known through Facebook. I took notice of each one of these bold women and loved them all so dearly that I wanted to sit on a carpet and look up at each and every one of them as they explained to me in detail the stories of their scars, freckles, and tattoos. Maybe that's what vodka and I will do for the next holiday.

Sincerity, I thought to myself when I ordered my third cocktail, *the twin sister of healing*.

Chapter 40

The Tears of His Mother

A few months after John's suicide, Garrett, who was seven years old at the time, asked me if I wanted to have his beloved doggy stuffed animal, Buster. He told me that Buster would make me stop crying at night.

I would have moments like these when my love for Garrett would fill me and warm me, but I couldn't take pleasure in any of it for more than a few seconds. I would think of how John's parents and grandparents also had these moments with John because they were so very good and nurturing and attentive to him as they raised him. I would think of how John was once a little boy like Garrett who chased lizards, nursed sick birds back to health, made mud pies with his sister, and possibly longed to comfort his mother with a stuffed animal. Along with the thoughts that John was once an innocent little boy, the guilt that lived in me and had attached itself to my insides would awaken from its dormant stage and make me nauseated.

I did this. I killed him. I am responsible for the tears of his mother.

When I couldn't talk myself out of the guilt, I'd send Garrett away to play video games, or I'd give him a chore to complete. Sometimes I'd just lock my bedroom door and tell him I was sick.

And I was sick. Sick with guilt and regret and responsibility and the fear that one day Garrett would succumb to the same fate John had, because love doesn't always equal salvation.

Chapter 41

Teal with Bright Yellow Stars

April 12, 2016

I dreamed that John's urn was put into a wooden coffin. The coffin was painted teal, with bright yellow stars. As it sat in the viewing room at Mead's Mortuary, I cried: bent over a table, snot running from my nose, and belly aching with pain. I wailed. Harder than I ever had in real life. I cried and cried for him. His mother was next to me, and I felt relief that she saw me cry.

Chapter 42

Five Shitty Things People Said to Me after His Suicide

1. "So when do you think you'll remarry?"

Gee, I don't know. Let me just finish up with this funeral nonsense, and then I'll get back to you on that.

2. "I guess you won't be getting any life insurance now…you know, it being suicide and all."

Thank you for that uplifting insight.

3. "You're not really alone, you know. You have Jesus."

Jesus can feel free to show up at any time now…

4. "You seem to have moved on a little too quickly. I don't think you're taking time to heal."

I really value your opinion on my life and my grieving process…How long has it been since your husband died? Oh, wait…What's that? Your husband is alive, and the two of you have been blissfully married for over a decade? Hm. OK. Thank you for your valuable advice. I will really think about this.

5. "It just sucks that the kids are going to be all screwed up now that they won't have a man around to help raise them."

Thank you for your confidence in my ability to parent my children without a man. When your kid is serving my little Harvard graduates their French fries at McDonalds, I will try not to act too smug.

Chapter 43

The F-Word

My third-favorite f-word is flowers, my second favorite f-word is food, and I'll let you guess what my first favorite f-word is.

Speaking of fucked, I think all of us widows can agree on the fact that our early postmortem memory banks are, well, fucked. I have no memory of making funeral arrangements ("funeral" is now my least favorite f-word), no idea if the kids even brushed their teeth that first year, and I truly have no clue why I woke up one morning during that first July of my widowhood wearing a bathrobe and black leather leggings in my front yard. What I do remember about those early days, though, are the flowers.

I love flowers! I sure as hell can't grow them myself, but a well-arranged bouquet of flowers delivered to my doorstep gives me about as much pride as I imagine one has when actually growing them in their own garden. I love flowers so much so that Lynnette and I compete monthly in something we call "the flower wars," in which we both see how many men and gay women we can convince with our charm to buy us flowers.

I love flowers.

I loved getting flowers at John's funeral because it meant that people were thinking of me. It also meant that they were acknowledging *to* me that there were no appropriate words to say in this situation. As the flower givers approached my pew at church the day of the funeral, the only form of communication they gave me was a sympathetic head tilt as they extended their floral-filled fists (I am having "fun" trying to "fit" as many "F" words into this post as "feasible"), and for this I am eternally grateful.

My favorite people in the world are people who know that the best thing to say to a widow at the funeral is *nothing*.

Where was I? Oh yes, fucking funeral flowers. Now that I have proven to all of you that I love flowers in general and that the funeral-specific flowers that I received were greatly appreciated, I need to tell you not to buy me flowers next time my husband kills himself (which is highly likely since I have had two husbands within a twelve-year span attempt suicide, hence why I am batshit crazy). Here's why:

Three days after John's funeral, I began to notice one of my lovely bouquets was wilting.

You know what else wilts? Dead people.

You know who was a dead person that week? The love of my life, John.

Well, as you can imagine, the sight of these wilting flowers sent me into hysterical sobs until the Valium kicked in nineteen minutes and fifteen seconds later. Once I was a properly sedated widow, I took the next logical step in my grief: I threw all the flowers away. I instantly felt guilty about this, as I knew the people who had bought them for me had the best of intentions, but I knew there simply was not enough Valium in the world to help me should I see another wilting flower.

Where did this flower-buying tradition come from? I'll bet it was the same people who invented shoelaces on toddler shoes. Neither is very logical. So what is logical then? What should we be giving to widows and widowers at the funeral?

I suggest the invention of something I like to call "the widow registry." A lot of us begin our marriages with registering for household items, so why not register for widowhood items as well? I can't tell you the pleasure I would have gotten had the funeral director said to me, "And to the right of our mahogany casket collection, we have the widow's shopping area. Here's your scanner and a glass of champagne." Now *that's* how I'd like for my mourning process to start!

Sometimes I fantasize about how amazing it would have been to be standing in front of my husband's urn at the funeral while a long line of people were handing me widow necessities and not saying a single. Damn. Word.

What would your widow registry have on it? Boxing gloves to punch your unempathetic family members with? Sleeping pills and an endless supply of wine? A coupon for free babysitting services until the end of time? How about a gift certificate to your local spa?

Michelle's widow registry would look something like this:

* gift cards for free pizzas to alleviate "the kids are going to starve to death because widow brain has made me forget how to cook" guilt,
* an endless supply of twenty- and hundred-dollar bills (wait… scratch the pizza gift cards if I get this),
* gallons of Bacardi 151 rum and Titio's Vodka with a side of air as a mixer,
* fifty-five-gallon drums of lotion-infused tissues,
* assorted fleece sweatpants and hoodies for the lazy three-year laundry-free mission I was about to embark on,
* Valium (funeral directors should be able to prescribe this),
* and boxes and boxes of condoms for all the one-night-stand grief sex I was about to be having in the days and years following the funeral.

Whatever is on your list, I want you to know that there is no statute of limitations on grief, and therefore, there is no statute of limitations on the widow registry. Yes, I know this amazing service does not really exist, but the idea of it, of treating yourself and allowing others to treat you, still can.

Widowhood sucks.

Even if you're thirty-five years into it, widowhood sucks. It will suck a little less when you don't have to cook for your kids and you have some warm fuzzy pants on during your bathroom-floor cry sessions.

What has happened to you is a tragedy. One of the few things religion and science both agree on is that humans were never meant to be alone, and yet, here you are. We were designed (or evolved) to be communal beings. We were meant to bond deeply, and so we have. And now that bond is irrevocably changed, and no matter how close a relationship your husband had with other people, they all most likely get to crawl into bed at night with their partners, while the widow (that's you!) is left with only the hope of finding the stray scent of her beloved on a pillow in the bed they once shared. If that doesn't warrant a free babysitter and an hour-long massage at a high-quality spa, I don't know what does.

Chapter 44

I Wore a White Dress to My Husband's Funeral

I wore a white dress to my husband's funeral, because it was March in the desert, and I was hot.

I wore a white dress to my husband's funeral, because I had lost eight pounds that week, and it was the only thing that fit.

I wore a white dress to my husband's funeral, because it made me feel pretty.

I wore a white dress to my husband's funeral, because being pretty was the only thing I knew to be true about myself that day.

I wore a white dress to my husband's funeral, because that dress was the last birthday present he would ever buy me.

I wore a white dress to my husband's funeral, because it was the last thing he saw me wearing.

I wore a white dress to my husband's funeral, because when I wore it, he said I looked like an angel.

I wore a white dress to my husband's funeral, because my husband didn't even believe in angels.

I wore a white dress to my husband's funeral, because fuck all of you who told me I should wear black.

I wore a white dress to my husband's funeral, because it made my breasts look big and perky for all the men who would hit on me at the wake.

I wore a white dress to my husband's funeral, because the material made for good and soft tissue for the noses, cheeks, and eyes of my children.

I wore a white dress to my husband's funeral, because my trembling hands wouldn't allow me to operate the buttons and zippers of my black dresses.

I wore a white dress to my husband's funeral, because its forgiving waistline makes it easy to kneel down in front of the toilet at the church and vomit.

I wore a white dress to my husband's funeral, because fuck expectations, traditional notions of grief, and making everyone else feel comfortable.

I wore a white dress to my husband's funeral, because Ho2 was in the second-to-last pew wearing black.

I wore a white dress to my husband's funeral, because I am done competing with her.

I wore a white dress to my husband's funeral, because I am pure, and she is tainted with my husband's blood.

I wore a white dress to my husband's funeral, because white is the color of a clean slate, of hope, of the bikini I was wearing when we first met, and of the color of my wedding dress.

I wore a white dress to my husband's funeral, because fuck adultery, fuck suicide, and fuck the loss of innocence my children have been subjected to.

Chapter 45

Was My Husband's Suicide a Choice?

"You have high markers for bipolar and depression," said our marriage counselor to John after looking over his paperwork, "but I can't formally diagnose you or prescribe meds; you need to go to a psychiatrist for that."

John crossed his arms, leaned back onto the therapist's sofa, and snorted in that familiar way that told me that he and his pride would not be making an appointment with a psychiatrist.

Men don't see psychiatrists. Men suck it up.

In this way, my husband chose suicide. I do not forgive him for this. He should have gotten help. I, too, was told I had high markers for major depressive disorder by our therapist. I promptly went to a doctor; tried diet, exercise, and vitamin supplements; and, when those failed, went on antidepressants. In this way, I chose life.

But maybe it was easier for me because I am a woman. Women see doctors. Women don't have to suck it up.

I do not forgive society for this double standard.

Two and a half years after this therapy appointment, John would attempt suicide two times before he succeeded Twice by carbon monoxide poisoning in his garage (he would admit this to me on the night he died) and once with a fatal shotgun bullet to his torso.

These attempts were not his choice. I know this because I've read his suicide note more times than I can count, and the author of that selfish, anger-laced letter was not the man I married. I know these attempts on his life were not his choice because I spent two hours on the phone with him, trying to talk the gun out of his hand. The voice on the phone that night was not my husband's.

The voice on the phone that night made me a believer in what the Holy Bible refers to as demonic possession. I recalled all the accounts in the New Testament of Jesus healing people from demon possession as I listened to John attempt to string sentences together that made no sense on the night of March 23, 2014.

As I listened to him on that awful night, I knew three things for sure.

One was that mental illness has always existed, and the authors of the Bible did not have "mental illness" in their vocabularies, so they referred to these people as "demon possessed."

Two, Jesus would not be saving my husband.

Three, I no longer believed in Jesus.

Not much has changed since biblical times. Although we now have "mental illness" in our vocabularies, we don't use it very much—or we use it but don't fully understand its meaning.

We call victims of suicide selfish. We tell ourselves and others that they made bad choices. I wonder if the demon possessed were called selfish.

There are very rare cases in which suicide is actually a choice.

Legally (or illegally, for that matter) assisted suicide for people with terminal illnesses is one. Suicide for the sake of honor, in cultures where choosing to die brings honor to one's tribe or family, is the other.

Outside of those two examples, I venture to say that the vast majority of suicide is *not* a choice.

The situation with my husband is a little more complicated, though. Did my husband choose suicide? Yes and no. Yes, he chose not to get help when he was told he had symptoms for two mental illnesses that could lead to suicide. Had he reached out for help, he might still be here…or he might still be dead. Plenty of people *do* reach out for help, and still they die by suicide. Or maybe when our therapist told him to see a psychiatrist, he was already too far gone, and his sick brain kept him from seeking help. Or maybe it was his pride. Or maybe it was society.

These are the questions I ponder at 1:00 a.m. while the nontraumatized people of the world get to sleep peacefully.

Did my husband John choose suicide? No. By the time he wrote that suicide note and loaded that shotgun, his brain had been overtaken by an illness. Saying that a mentally ill person *chose* suicide is like saying my maternal grandmother *chose* not to feed herself when her cancer spread to her brain, and she lost her fine and gross motor skills.

Do me a favor: the next time you see or hear the word "suicide," replace it with the term "brain cancer," and see how your perception of its victims and survivors change.

John's sick brain made the choice to fire that gun, but my husband did not. My husband was not merely a brain, and I resent those who treat his legacy as such. John was a unique and precious soul, and that soul no longer existed as it once did. It was encased within a sick body.

While I will always be conflicted about whether or not John's suicide was a choice, and whether or not it could have been prevented, I am not at all conflicted when I say this: *no one has the right to tell me John's suicide was a choice.*

No one.

The implication of saying this to me, a suicide widow, is that my husband chose to leave the kids and me (which only makes us feel more shitty…so thanks for that) and that my husband was a selfish person. Maybe he was, and maybe he wasn't. Either way, I'm allowed to think and say this about *my* husband. *You* are not.

I am sickened when I see people attacking the loved ones of those who have lost their battles with depression, Post Traumatic Stress Disorder bipolar disorder, and other undiagnosed mental illnesses. Your opinions are self-serving, pretentious, and, of course, "well intended."

You're not allowed to voice an opinion to someone who has slept in their dead spouse's shirt in hopes that their skin cells might still be on the tattered fabric.

You're not allowed to voice an opinion to someone who has had to tell their young children, "Daddy did something called 'suicide.'"

You're not allowed to voice an opinion to someone who has picked out clothing for a corpse to wear in a coffin.

You're not allowed to voice an opinion to someone who has ever had to check the "widowed" box on paperwork.

So what are you allowed to do?

You're allowed to shut. The. Fuck. Up.

Chapter 46

Why I Stayed

People always ask me why I stayed. "If my husband ever cheated," they say with so much confidence, "I'd leave in a heartbeat!" The thing about heartbeats, though, is that they have different rhythms when your heart has been shattered. Their beats become prolonged, then sometimes staccato, and almost always inaudible. Broken hearts make decisions that whole hearts cannot fathom.

To articulate the answer to this very important question, I searched my stack of journals that had served as my lifeboats during the affair years.

I am exhausted. How much longer, God? Will I do all of this work, and he'll still leave? Will I do all of this work, and he'll stay, and we'll have an awful marriage? What happened to the man I married? Was he all a lie? Or was that really him, and he has changed into this horrible creature? I am a widow. The man I loved and knew is dead.

I wrote this two years before John's physical death. And then, on the Christmas before his suicide a few years later, I wrote:

My babies. My loves. I have failed them. It's too late now. I should've left John years ago when I found the sex videos. Did I misinterpret the signs? Was God really wanting me to stay in my marriage? If so, why do I feel so strongly now that I should leave? Why now? Why not then?

I had spent more than two years toiling over a marriage that not only wasn't going to work out but that would also end with me becoming a suicide widow. Was all this time, prayers, counseling, crying, and competitive fucking done in vain?

(Competitive fucking: *verb*. All the wild-ass sex you have with your husband once you find out he's a porn-addicted adulterer. Used to convince yourself that you are better in bed than all the porn girls. And the real-life affair girls. Also see: delusional.)

Why did I stay after the discovery of my husband's affairs?

I could tell you that I stayed because I was a Christian at the time, and Christian wives of atheist husbands are encouraged (read: guilted and shamed) into staying in marriages to win their husbands for Christ. I could also tell you that I stayed for money and fear of my small-town reputation, which is partially true and nothing to be ashamed of. I could explain to you the physical pains that plagued my body each and every time I thought about telling my kids that Mommy and Daddy were divorcing, but no.

Those are simple, superficial answers that make me comfortable, which means they are not the whole truth and nothing but the truth, so help me, Beyoncé. The thing about the truth is that it really does set you free, but first, it will make you uncomfortable, possibly sick, and almost always embarrassed.

The truth is that I stayed with John because I was in love with him. I am cringing and clenching my jaw as I type this. What a disgrace to female empowerment I am! I viewed my husband's sex tapes, scrolled through hundreds of incriminating pictures, e-mails, and phone records, listened as he told me that not only did he not love me, but also that he never had, and…

I.
Still.
Loved.
Him.

And not only did I still love him, I loved him so much, I stayed for more than two years after the affair revelations while he tortured me with more lies, refusal to take any of the blame, and, worst of all, a deliberate, physical withdrawal from me and the kids.

Maybe the real question here should be: Was I in love, or was I a fucking martyr? That question is easy; I was both. There is always an element of martyrdom when it comes to true love.

There I go avoiding the "Why did you stay?" question again. Another truth—besides my pathetic ability to love a man who rejected me—is that it is very difficult for me to discuss the love I had for John. Hating him is easier, recalling all the bad things about him keeps him close to me while also keeping him far away, and focusing on his infidelities makes my grief about his suicide more bearable. One of my New Year's resolutions should be to write three full blogs about good memories I have of John when we were in love...*and we were in love* at one time, no matter what his sick brain believed. Until then, though, I will say this.

I did not stay married for my kids, or for my God, or for my financial stability. What it comes down to for me is that I stayed for love. That rush of chemicals that coursed through my brain every time my husband came home from work. That calming feeling I'd get when we'd make eye contact from across the room at a boring family gathering. His unshaven face on my cheeks...and, OK, on my inner thighs, too. The way he looked when he held the kids. The way he *got me*, the real me. The me who, if he were still here today, he would just *get*, even after the metamorphosis that widowhood had forced upon me.

Love doesn't end just because it is unrequited. It doesn't end with sex tapes from whores and the throwing of cups in the garage at 11:00 p.m. on a Thursday. It doesn't even end with the removal of wedding rings and a self-inflicted shotgun wound through the torso. Sometimes love doesn't end, even when you want it to. And then sometimes love ends when it ends without any rhyme or reason to it.

I won't say that I fully understand the love I had for the man I thought I would grow old with. I won't say that I fully understand the new love that I developed for my husband since he died. I will say, though, that a few years and a few paragraphs ago, I was ashamed to admit to my love for him, but I no longer am as I finish this blog. I loved him. I stayed with him because of this. I worked those last few years of our marriage to save him, and when I failed, he took his life, but none of the love or work was done in vain or in opposition to female empowerment. My ability to love John even when he had stopped loving me, my ability to love him still even after his death, is how I know that hope and strength still exist inside me, even on the days when I can't feel them.

Chapter 47

From John's Blog: Sleepless Morning Rant

March 6, 2014 eighteen days before his suicide

Ok again another sleepless night. I am the only person that I know that can take a sleeping pill and only get 4 hours of sleep. But then again I am the only person I know that can be on antidepressants and still cry yourself to sleep every night. I keep begging god for mercy but that hasn't happened yet. Either my sins are too great and I deserve this punishment or he's just a bit too busy right now. Sorry my morning rant is over. Hope you all have a good day.

Chapter 48

Rage Widow and Her French Fries

Can you sell an opened box of condoms on Craigslist? How about used, fishnet thigh-highs? Wait, no, maybe I should keep those, because they look great with my leather zipper dress. Wait. I guess I don't have anywhere to wear my leather zipper dress now that I have recently chosen to give up on men indefinitely. That last sentence is misleading, since I actually gave up on men somewhere around the time I listened to my husband's screams as he shot himself over the phone with me. Let's rephrase that: I am giving up men. I am giving up *on* them, and I am giving *them up*, officially.

I am giving up on ever finding one who can handle my level of crazy, and I am giving up dating, talking to, or even texting their species—except for a few assorted crazy widowers on social media, the gay ones, and male relatives who haven't blocked me from social media yet.

Why the sudden change of heart (or rather, vagina) after two and a half years of grief sex, sex grief, rage dating, dating about rage, and dating seven men at a time like a female version of Hugh Heffner (only less adorable)? I blame my wedding ring.

The week before Christmas, I was having my annual "I'm the reason my in-laws don't get to see their son at Christmas" guilty crying sesh on the bathroom floor when I got the sudden urge to fish my wedding rings out from the abyss under my sink.

My rage at John had been dissipating for months, ever since the release of my first book, and with this decline, a decline in my sex drive ensued. Something about its publication made me feel like that rage-filled chapter of my life needed to be over, and so it had been for the most part, but I needed something to really remind me consistently that John and I had been in love so that I didn't hate him.

Putting my wedding rings back on that night after almost three years of their absence from my left hand felt like a warm blanket, and this action solidified my transition from Crazy Rage Widow to Appropriately Sad (yet still somehow crazy) Widow. Or so I thought. While I haven't had any noticeable anger during my waking hours since putting my ring on, I've been having the most vivid, psychopathic, angry dreams you can imagine.

I am so very Zen during the day (or as Zen as one can be in a house with five kids, Guilt Bunny, and a Lynnette), but deep down, I must not be.

Last night, for instance, I dreamed I was having violent sex (his penis was a switchblade) on a bathroom floor with a man whom I will just refer to as Number Forty-Five (yes, the same Number Forty-Five from my first book) while yelling at Ho1, "You're a worthless piece of shit! John never loved you! He was only playing house with you! It's me he killed himself over!" Then I watched as John sat in an overstuffed armchair and refused to back me up.

How dare he not back me up while I am being taken on the bathroom floor by Number Forty-Five and his knife dick!

So I started yelling at him, too. I started yelling vulgar, crude, profanities that Awake Michelle is even too fucking freaked out about to type in this blog. OK, so maybe I'm not as "over" the rage as I thought I was.

Two nights ago in my dreams, I was boxing. The speed bags were Ho2's breasts. I punched them until they sprayed blood on my face. I used this blood as makeup.

A week ago, I dreamed Ho2 had put her and John's sex tapes on Facebook to try to gain sympathy from people by proving that she and John were closer and had better sex than John and I did. I promptly went to her house, pulled her toddler out of their crib, threw the baby in the air, and shot her with John's shotgun. Then I laughed and ate French fries.

Is anyone still reading this, or did I lose you after the bloody makeup and baby murdering? I realize Rage Widow and her French fries might be a bit much for some to handle.

I am sick. Yet during the day lately, I feel so damn healthy. I gaze lovingly at my engagement ring and think about how the night John gave it to me, I slept with it on even though it hadn't been sized yet and kept waking up every few minutes to make sure it hadn't fallen off of my finger. I tear up with pity when I think of John being so depressed that last year of his life and forget to remember how in that last year he'd also become violent. I leave texts from men unanswered; I decline booty calls and romantic dinner propositions. I (gasp!) pray.

I still have my nightly cocktail, but it's been reduced to one, followed by some one-on-one time with my Snuggie, hot tea, and a book.

But then I go to sleep, and I'm Rage Widow again. (Does anyone else think Rage Widow would be a badass name for a superhero?)

What is going on here? Is it possible that true rage, like true love, never really goes away? Does our love and our hate for our deceased loved ones carry on for the remainder of our lives? Should I stop thinking my rage will ever go away and just accept that it will always manifest in my life somehow? Should I, too, accept this about my love for John? And more importantly, can I channel this hatred into grief sex and my love for him into yoga or something so that I can have a banging body? Having rage dreams rarely ever results in an orgasm.

I just want widowhood to be over now. I am ready for this life to be done. I want to wake up and find that my grief has vanished. I'm waving the white flag, Universe! I surrender! Do you fucking hear me? I'm done! Make it stop. Please, in the name of Beyoncé, just make it cease.

The rage, the voids inside of deeper voids, the guilt.

My. Dear. God. The. *Guilt*.

The regrets that I regret. The regrets that I don't regret that I feel guilty about not regretting. My innocence that was lost with a shotgun—I'm gonna need that back now. The images of my children riding on John's back. Please, someone erase this memory specifically.

Tell me this has all been one of my violent nightmares. Tell me I no longer have anything or anyone to hate.

Chapter 49

Band-Aids

For the third day in a row, I was lying comatose on the left side of my king-sized bed among the gray flannel sheets and yellow feather duvet. Three half-empty teacups without coasters sat carelessly and dangerously close to the edge of my nightstand. It was Thanksgiving of 2011, just a few months postaffair, and we had to go to my in-laws' and act like everything was fine. I hadn't showered since Monday morning. Garrett, just five years old at the time, entered my fortress of depression without knocking, wearing nothing but Superman briefs and one sock (his sister's) that went up to his knee. In his hand was a plastic toy doctor's kit. Neither of us said anything, not even a greeting, as he opened the kit at the end of my bed and put the toy stethoscope around his neck and then into his ears.

He started his examination at my forehead, after he moved my unwashed bangs aside. Then he listened to my chest, which he had to listen to twice because of the thickness of my stained terrycloth robe. Next was my elbow, which he labored to get to under my heavy, lethargic arm. Then were my kneecaps, as he rolled up the too-large-for-my-frame polyblend plaid bottoms that I'd had on since I got home from work on Monday. Finally, he listened to my feet through the rubbery padding of my slipper socks.

I wanted the sweetness of that moment to warm the chills out of me, but I knew it wouldn't. I wanted the wonder of his imagination to inspire me, but I knew it couldn't. I wanted to be the playful, nurturing mother he deserved, but I knew I was not.

Examination complete, and still silent, his small hands pulled his coveted Thomas the Tank Engine Band-Aids from the kit. He placed one on my right kneecap, one on my left ankle, and lastly one over my heart, taking extra care to make sure it stuck to my robe. He kissed my cheek, said, "All better now, Mommy, 'K?" and then he left. I didn't even cry.

I don't have any memories of Thanksgiving that year except for the dream I had that night.

Sinking. That night in my dreams, I was sinking. I was stuck in quicksand while everyone I knew and loved was just inches away, waving. I fought the fast-moving thickness at first, reaching out for loved ones' hands until I realized the inevitability of the sand and succumbed to it for lack of a better option.

Chapter 50

Stand

I wish confronting the other woman was like it is in the movies. If it was, I would have had a hair, makeup, and wardrobe team with me to make my first confrontation with Ho1 much more glamorous. In real life, though, what I had instead of a glam squad was the fucking wind and a hangover that would have made Charles Bukowski proud.

Am I allowed to make jokes about a dead guy? I don't know. I was born without tact, but what I do know is that I hate the wind, and I hate hangovers, both of which I encountered a lot of when I lived in that little town in the Mojave Desert in 2011.

Also during this time period, I grew to hate people, animals, work, anything that didn't have vodka in it, and Fridays. Dear God, I hated Fridays during the affair years of my marriage! Not only was Friday grocery day (a task made almost impossible when your brain has been overtaken by depression), but on Fridays I was also required to wear a logo T-shirt to represent the school where I worked, which conveniently is also the same school my children attended (at least one thing in my life at this time was working to my advantage). Not that I am against cartoon bear mascots or anything, but a school-logo T-shirt is definitely not my best outfit…They don't make cleavage-bearing school-spirit shirts for whatever the reason.

On this particular Friday, I had managed to mask my hangover with makeup and false eyelashes, but after waking up to a seasonal desert sandstorm at 3:00 a.m., I knew my hair didn't stand a chance. It was decided that morning that I would sport my go-to messy-bun look. Despite my messy bun, though, I'm sure the kids and I appeared to outsiders to be the perfect little family entering the grocery store on that windy, chilly morning. We were all wearing matching blue-bear shirts to support our school, with smiles on our faces to mask the truth: we were secretly imploding.

My son's toenails hadn't been clipped in months because my depression just wouldn't allow me to. I remember how they kept breaking off at school when he played soccer at recess, prompting the school nurse to remind me (again), in as nonjudgmental a tone as possible, that they need to be trimmed soon. I had also just had a recent conference with his teacher about how he wouldn't stop crying in class out of nowhere, and Isabelle's bedtime anxiety and nightmares were getting increasingly worse each night. She may have actually been sleeping less than me at that point, prompting a conference with *her* teacher about how she kept falling asleep during reading time.

I know for sure now that even without words, kids know what is happening. Even with all of my flowery words about how Mommy and Daddy were just fine and how Mommy was just a little sick from the flu, I shielded my children from nothing. I regret not sitting them down and telling them the meaning of an affair and that their dad was guilty of seven years of them. Humanity sucks, and the sooner children are made aware (in an age-appropriate way, of course) of how truly sucky humanity is, the sooner they can reconcile this disappointment and begin the natural journey that occurs after this epiphany: the journey to discover the flip side of sucky humanity, the benevolent, unbelievably love-filled one. They can't seek this out for themselves if they don't first see the shit.

Show your children the shitty side of humanity, or life will show it to them for you.

Where was I? Oh yes, the damn grocery store in a damn sandstorm. I don't even know where to start with how much I was imploding at this time in my life—the daily shakes from alcohol withdrawal, the chronic yeast infections from constant sex with John to convince him that I was better than the porn girls and his affair partners, the outline of my exposed femur from the drastic weight I'd lost, my teeth coming loose from all the vomiting, the chunks of my hair falling out from vitamin deficiencies.

The collateral physical damage of infidelity is far-reaching and perhaps the most selfish part of this whole damn thing.

As I mentioned earlier, this, of course, was the day I saw Hol for the first time since seeing her naked in the videos I found in John's e-mail months earlier. I robotically grabbed a cart and instructed the kids to hold on to either side. When the automatic doors opened, there she was at register six, practically glowing in the fluorescent lights with her head down, looking through her designer wallet.

Rich cunt.

It was like seeing a celebrity. It was like seeing a celebrity you hated but also found to be very beautiful, like Pamela Anderson in the '90s. It was like seeing a celebrity you hated but also found to be very beautiful but that you also wanted to kill because she had fucked your husband.

It was a very complicated millisecond.

I instinctively retreated back out of the doors that hadn't closed yet behind me, and my hand went straight to my messy bun. There was no hope of doing anything with that rat's nest on the top of my head, and I knew it. I was momentarily paralyzed, as I stood outside the grocery store in the wind, by the multiple insecurities she had planted in me months earlier. She had unknowingly been watering these seeds of insecurity daily, every single time she posted a picture of herself on her social media, which I had been stalking for months.

What was infidelity like before social media? I would really like to know.

My split-second glance at Hol had assured me that she was every bit as perfect looking as she was on her social media and in my nightmares that she made cameos in nightly. Her hair appeared to be professionally styled, her makeup practically airbrushed, and if there was such a thing as Prada Business-Time Barbie, she had the outfit to match.

Then there was me: frumpy housewife/part-time special-needs aide with crazy Sicilian hair and too much makeup in all the wrong spots. One kid with jagged toenails snagging his socks and one kid with bags under her eyes from lack of sleep.

I had a choice to make:

A. I could hide outside and hope she used the other door to exit.
B. I could hide outside and ram her with my cart when she came out of the exit door in front of me.
C. I could run for my life (we didn't need those pesky little things called "groceries" anyway).
D. I could go back in, look her in the eyes, and claim my territory.

But first, lip gloss. What is it about lip gloss that just empowers me? I don't know, but it made my decision for me in less than a second that day.

I am sorry to tell you that lip gloss and I did not choose option B. Keep in mind, this was 2011 Michelle, not 2016 Michelle. The 2016 version of Michelle would be typing this blog in a maximum-security prison right now.

I really like 2016 Michelle.

I pushed my cart inside and stopped right there in the entryway. I planted my feet next to the sales-ad rack and complimentary antibacterial cart wipes. With one hand on my hip and one hand on my cart, I glared boldly and openly at Ho1, willing her to look at me.

I was shaking uncontrollably with fear.

She *will* visually acknowledge me and my children's existence here on earth.

She *will* take some sort of responsibility in the devastation of my life instead of (according to her Instagram) dressing up in something cute and going to a damn party every fucking day of the week.

She *will* at the very least be made uncomfortable by my presence.

At one point, something inside me started to talk me out of my statue confrontation (as I now refer to it) when a lady behind me with her cart said, "Excuse me," twice, and I refused to budge. But then another part of me decided that you just can't bargain with a crazy, hungover, sleep-deprived affair victim, so I just stood.

I stood, and I stared, and I trembled.

"Mom, why aren't we moving?" asked my daughter. "Are you OK?"

"I'm looking for something..." I responded, without breaking my stare.

Just then, Ho1 looked up from her wallet. Our eyes locked. *"Yeah, bitch, I've seen the video of your clitoris and labia, and there is definitely cellulite on both of them, you worthless whore,"* I said with my eyes. She broke the stare immediately.

As I stood firmly and watched her fumble with her bag of groceries and purse, before fleeing through the farthest exit she could find, relief flooded over me. Wait, no, it wasn't exactly relief. Pride, maybe? There was an element of humor to it, too, though, as I watched her run away with her tail tucked between her legs. It was the opposite of pity, whatever that is, and it was the first flicker of fight inside me, and all I did was stand and stare. Oh, and tremble with fear, too. Did I mention the severity of the shaking? I was scared as fuck, but I stood anyway.

Sometimes the strongest thing we can do amid the depression, the exhaustion, the anger, and the hangovers is just to stand.

I stood and stared, and that was my fight. Something as simple as this can be your fight, too. We like to think that meaningful fights involve fists, yelling, blood, and trophies, but more times than not in this life, the battles we wage are done by simply standing. I stood and declared to myself that I was done being a doormat, that my victimhood was about to come to an end. Even though I spent that night facedown in my bedroom, crying into the carpet, the few seconds that I *had* stood that day could not be erased. Each battle I faced after this day was built upon the few seconds that I stood, unflinching in front of that worthless ho-bag.

In the years that followed this day, I did a lot of standing.

I stood above my children as they slept, and I rehearsed a speech in my head that began with the words, "Last night, while you were sleeping, Daddy died…"

I stood on a stage at my husband's funeral and gave a speech about love and gratitude in front of Ho2, who sat toward the back of the church with her husband's arm around her.

I stood in line at the social security office, sick to my stomach, wondering if I'd qualify for enough benefits to keep paying the mortgage.

I stood over my husband's headstone and watched my children decorate it with flowers, stuffed animals, and bottles of soda.

I stood as I told the moving men where to put the furniture in our new home in San Diego.

And then I stood in front of audiences at launch parties and book signings to celebrate and promote a book that I wrote about grief and love and despair.

I would not have had the strength to do these things if messy bun, lip gloss, and I had not first stood in the entryway of that grocery store in the middle of that damn sandstorm.

Chapter 51

My Husband's Last Day on Earth

It is my husband's last day on earth, but I don't know this yet. What I do know is that I am annoyed. It is March 23, 2014, and I wake up, like I have every morning for the last fifty-five days since I left him, to a text message.

Is it going to be an angry text or an ass-kissing text? Drunk or sober? I wonder what my crazy, soon-to-be-ex has in store for me today.

As I rub my morning eyes and unlock my phone, the light from the screen burns, so I squint.

"I'd like to change the oil in your car today," it reads.

Ass-kissing. Good. Maybe I can get him to schedule another appointment with the divorce lawyers, since I had to cancel our previous one due to my panic-attack-side-of-the-road-vomit fest on the way to our last appointment.

Later, as I park the car in the driveway of the home we once shared, I see my husband step outside into the unfiltered desert sunlight. His appearance isn't shocking; it is disturbing. How could he have changed so much since yesterday, when I had picked the kids up from him?

He is wearing a white T-shirt, crisp like he'd just taken it out of the Hanes package. It doesn't have a pocket. He has a fresh haircut, and after years of letting his beard grow unkempt, he is as clean-shaven as he was on our wedding day. His jeans fit loosely around his hips, magnifying how much weight he's lost. His skin looks so pale in comparison to the dark bags under his eyes, and where are his glasses?

As if he hears my thoughts, he brings his right hand up to his face and fastens the prescription sunglasses to his weathered face.

As he descends the staircase, he is sexy, shoeless, and calm.

Not just calm, but something else. Something I cannot identify. Something that becomes magnified as I come closer to him. It's like, peaceful—but more. He looks like how I imagined heaven to feel when I was young and stupid enough to believe in heaven. He looks broken *and* healed. Tired *and* rested. Defeated, maybe? I don't know. He looks like a stranger, and yet he also looks like an old friend.

He meets me at the bottom of the staircase to exchange the car keys. I sit.

"Do you need me to pack anything for the kids' field trip this week? They're so excited that their daddy is going..."

"I like your new haircut; where'd you get it cut?"

"That bottom stair seems loose. Can you repair it before the kids come over?"

I'm stalling, I'm stalling, and I don't know why. Something in me just wants us to be normal again, to discuss the minutiae of everyday life instead of the complications of turning our one life into two. It's quiet for a minute until I ask him if he has found a home yet for the dogs. I make a joke about the new owners having to deal with their literal shit.

My husband laughs, and then immediately his face contorts, and tears quickly stream down his face. His polarized emotions are familiar to me. In those early days after his affairs, I was in so much pain that even laughter brought me to tears. A swelling of tenderness for him, for the man I once got into a fight for at a racetrack when I was six months pregnant because someone called him an asshole, begins its uprising. I want to put my hands on his face and draw his head in against my chest. I want to stroke his fresh haircut and whisper to him that I understand.

I understand how the pain is so deep that even laughter hurts. I understand being unable to eat. I understand the nightmares, night sweats, and nights waking up in a puddle of your own tears. I understand the teeth grinding, the sharp and sudden chest pains, and the inability to control racing negative thoughts.

I stifle my desires to soothe him. It's not my job. He's had two and a half years to admit that his affairs were his fault. He's had two and a half years to apologize to me. He's had two and a half years to get on medication to treat his anxiety.

No, it is no longer my job to comfort him.

I'd spent two and a half years being blamed for his unfaithfulness, his rage, and his paranoias. I'd spent two and a half years waiting for him to empathize with me and tell me that he was sorry. I'd spent two and a half years manipulating him with niceties, sex, and food to try to convince him to get psychiatric help.

I'd spent two and a half years putting this man above my children. I'll never get those years back, and I know it. Their birthdays, skinned knees, spelling tests, and footed-pajama days happened in front of my very eyes, and I missed them because of this man. I will always hate him for this.

Even as I purposely hate him to keep myself from comforting him, I don't want to leave my spot on the staircase. I've been cold for months, and now, sitting here in my husband's shadow, I feel warm. How can it be that underneath all of this hate, there is still love?

> *We will get back together one day*, I decide internally. *We will be like one of those divorced couples that still has sex every once in a while. When enough time has passed, and he is once again the man I married, we will get back together.*

A vision of us both in white, getting remarried in a wheat field, flashes in my head.

In nine hours, I will get my husband's suicide note via text message.

In eleven hours, I will listen to my husband scream as he shoots himself while he is on the phone with me.

But I don't know this yet. All I know is that I have to leave my warm spot on the staircase. I have to go do my hair and put on my face. I have two dates to go on today.

This is an unpublished excerpt from my first book, *Boys, Booze, and Bathroom Floors*. It was supposed to be between chapters 3 and 4, but I removed it during the final round of editing. Why? Because of shame. I was ashamed to admit that I had been on dates while my husband was in the final stages of losing his sanity and his life.

Have you ever stopped to think about the fear someone has as they load the shotgun that will terminate their existence? What about the anger? What about the excitement? What about the shame?

TheShame.

Have you ever stopped to really think about the shame? Guilt is feelings of displeasure for something that you did. Shame is feelings of displeasure for *who you are* because of what you did. It is the conception of self-hatred, the seed of suicide. Shame killed my husband. As did anger and fear and excitement, but it all started when his brain began telling him that his actions weren't bad; *he* was bad.

Shame has the potential to kill me, like it did him. I am not above suicide. I've had moments, usually involving a man and a bathroom floor, when I have understood John's inclination to load that gun. To write that suicide text. To abandon his children. And it is in those moments when I choose to fight in the only way I know how: with words and with living.

So many people in my life want me to fight with prayers, activism, and silence. So many people want me to not fight at all. Fuck them. Each time

I write or say something that is true, something that offends people, each time I give in and go home with a bartender and then make a joke about it on Facebook, each time I admit my parenting pitfalls, my hatred toward God, or publish a blog about how I was dating on the day my husband ended his life, I am fighting shame.

    I am fighting a fight that John lost, a fight that I'm not even sure he attempted to fight. I will continue to fight shame every day by living and writing honestly, unapologetically, and with great love, admiration, and kindness for myself. These are all of the things that John could not do, and in living this way, I honor him.

Chapter 52

Bathit Crazy Joy

It was the kind of Christmas when the kids and I could only listen to *The Marshall Mathers LP*. I don't know if it was the coldest December in San Diego history or if it just felt that way to me. I couldn't get enough hot tea and blankets. It also felt dark, darker than the last two Christmases we had spent living here since John's suicide almost three years ago. Yes, it felt dark—and sad. It was that type of sad that I knew wasn't simply sadness; it was the type of sad that I get at the onset of a major depressive episode. I had been fighting off this type of sadness since John's death, afraid to really feel it for fear that this time I would not recover from it. And my kids didn't need two dead parents.

I had recently broken up with a man whom I had wasted six months of my life on. At the end of it all, he still never knew my last name. On the same day I realized he didn't know my last name after all that time, I decided to just go ahead and walk myself down to rock bottom with a bottle of vodka and a mission to find my and John's wedding rings. When I found them among his grandmother's collection of costume jewelry in the darkest part of the bathroom cabinet and didn't cry, I knew my impending depressive episode was going to be bad.

I had reached this point once before, when the depression was so deep that I couldn't cry. It took me six months, a hospital visit, and three different kinds of meds to stabilize me. I did not have the luxury of another major depressive episode this time. I was now a solo parent, a solo parent who knew that life and brain chemicals don't really give a shit about my lack of luxuries.

I put the familiar yet foreign bands on my ring finger for a moment and let myself think about the first time John put them each on my finger. Still no tears. I thought about how he'd confessed to me that he would take off his ring and leave it in the car when he went to meet one of his affair partners. Still no tears. I thought about how he had lost his original wedding band during one of these encounters and got a new one without me ever knowing until just before he shot himself. Still no tears. I thought about how I had once hoped to give my ring to my great-grandchildren when I became old enough to start thinking about who should get which of my possessions when I die. Still no tears.

Then I had to pack. In keeping on with my new "run-the-hell-away" widowhood holiday tradition, I had reserved a cabin for the kids and I to spend the few days in before Christmas. I don't have many memories of that trip. Just another blurry, numb holiday-avoidance attempt interrupted by a few photo opportunities and contests between the kids and me to see who had the most Eminem lyrics memorized.

We spent Christmas morning at my parents' house in my hometown. The same hometown John and I had once made a life in. The same hometown he'd had all his affairs in. The same hometown he had died in. By 10:00 a.m. on Christmas morning, I had to leave. I wanted to be back in my safe, cold, dark San Diegan haven, and I couldn't wait one more minute. The kids wanted to stay with their grandparents for a few more days. Two and a half hours later, I arrived back to San Diego and began to unload my things into an empty house. It was silent. Too silent.

This is where I need to introduce you to something called a Guilt Bunny. When John shot himself, I suffered from a very common delusion that most widowed parents have: I thought I could fix my kids' grief. One of the ways I attempted to bandage their massive dead-dad laceration was with a pet bunny. They had always wanted one, and about two seconds after I uttered the words, "Last night while you were sleeping, Daddy died," I made the brilliant and well-thought-out decision to expand our family with a gray dwarf bunny named Nibbles.

The look of delight on the kids' faces alleviated my "I couldn't save your dad" guilt for about seven seconds, and then every day after this I was hit with the realization that I had one more thing in my life I was obligated to take care of. Still, this bunny was adored by my children. Some days she roamed freely around the living room, jumping into my lap for attention, and other days she lived in the pseudo-wild of the makeshift chicken coop I had built for her once upon a time when I was feeling energetic.

That Christmas, I was devoid of all energy. I didn't even have the energy to think thoughts. My brain felt hollow, and it was all I could do to just inhale and exhale. I wanted to die, but my arms were too heavy to lift a pill bottle, fashion a noose, or load a gun. I wanted to run away and hide on an island, but my feet were too heavy to walk. So I just sat there in the silence of my living room. The silence…

Nibbles the bunny was always up to something—spinning her salt wheel, suckling from her water bottle, or jumping from her perch. I knew before I looked outside that she was gone for good. Of course she was gone. It was the most depressing Christmas of all time, so naturally, Nibbles the bunny had gone all Shawshank Redemption on me.

I'm having trouble putting into words the emotional reaction I had to this. It wasn't that I was so attached to this bunny, and now she was gone, and I missed her. It wasn't the thought of that poor, defenseless, pampered bunny running around our neighborhood in the rain—have I mentioned yet that it had been raining for two weeks? It wasn't the thought that she had surely been a very decadent Christmas meal for a lucky neighborhood dog. No. It was the thought of telling the kids that she was gone. The instant I saw the empty bunny coop, I started having clear and precise flashbacks of the looks on Isabelle's and Garrett's faces when I told them about John's suicide. The way their eyes widened while the rest of their faces fell. The way their chins began to quiver along with the rest of their bodies. The way I saw their childhood leave them through each teardrop that made contact with my shirt. After telling them about their dad, the only way I could still be their mother was to completely disassociate from this memory—and so I had, for more than two years, until the night that Nibbles, the motherfucking Guilt Bunny, went missing.

I am not exaggerating when I say this was the hardest I have ever cried in my life, and it was the longest, too. The violent wailing went on for nearly eight hours. I had decided, while vomiting in the shower, that if I could not pull myself together around hour twelve, I would check myself into a mental hospital. Seriously. Somewhere in the middle of this, Lynnette came home and watched helplessly from the staircase as I wandered around, hysterically coughing in the kitchen in between going outside and, like a lunatic, calling out to the escaped bunny who had probably been missing for two days.

I wanted John. I wanted my husband. I wanted my old life, when my sanity wasn't hanging on the presence of a dwarf bunny. I hadn't asked for this life. I didn't deserve it, and here I was, living it while the other women who had affairs with my husband (and therefore aided in his mental decline and suicide) were spending Christmas with their living husbands and their children whose innocence was still intact.

When the sun rose the day after Christmas, I was in the backyard, sleep-deprived and dehydrated, wearing my tiger-striped, fleece onesie. Around 4:00 a.m., the relentless tears had been replaced by a pit in my stomach. I was going to have to tell the kids that Nibbles was gone. They would be home in a few days, and sometime today, they would ask me to send them a picture of the bunny playing with the new toys that we had put in her stocking.

Lynnette and I spent hours scheming that morning about what to do. We considered buying a similar bunny but knew the kids were too smart to fall for this, so we began to come up with ways to lessen the blow and therefore minimize the look of sorrow on their faces when I told them that Nibbles was gone for good so that I would not end up being triggered again. It was decided that I needed to do everything I could possibly do to prove to the kids that I had searched for that bunny. This would lessen the guilt I had and possibly make them hate me a little less for not letting them bring Nibbles on our Christmas vacation with us like they had begged me to do five days ago.

I was showing a picture of Nibbles to the third neighbor before I realized that I was still in my tiger-striped, onesie, footed pajamas. By the time I got home, the neighborhood was alive with the first sunshine we'd seen in weeks, and with that, the neighbor kids were all out in the streets and sidewalks playing with their new Christmas toys while their parents, coffee mugs in hand, looked on.

Next, I decided to empty out the vegetable bin of our refrigerator in the yard. Yes, I was going to put vegetables on the perimeter of our house to lure the bunny (and all the feral bunnies within a two-mile radius) back to me. If she didn't come back, then at least the kids would see the vegetables and know that their mother had tried everything she could to find the damn Guilt Bunny.

When randomly scattering the vegetables around the yard didn't satiate the guilt pit in my stomach, I got down on my hands and knees in our front yard and began to strategically place the wilting vegetation into a trail that would lead Nibbles back to her coop. I sat up and leaned back to admire the trail I had just created.

Now, I'm not much of a believer in supernatural activities ever, and at this point in my life, I definitely did not believe in the existence of God or angels, so I am just as skeptical as you are going to be when you read this next part: at that moment, as I sat up to look at the vegetable trail, Nibbles the motherfucking Guilt Bunny, fell from the sky and into my lap.

At first I thought I had hallucinated her. Then I thought that it must be some other bunny, but when she looked up at me with a look on her face that said, "Hey, bitch, why you putting my organic romaine lettuce in the dirt?" I knew it was her. I grabbed on to her as she tried to leave my lap to have a snack, and sobbed uncontrollably while whisper-yelling, "You stupid motherfucker!"

Me in my tiger-striped onesie calling a bunny a motherfucker is one of the main reasons Lynnette and I don't get invited to neighborhood parties anymore.

I am not exaggerating at all when I say to you that this was the happiest moment of my life. Happier than the moment my kids were born, happier than looking into John's eyes on our wedding day as I said my vows, happier than the moment Lynnette and I spent dancing in a mud pit at Gay Pride, happier than the moment when I discovered chocolate cheesecake with an Oreo crust, and even happier than the moment I learned firsthand (ahem) what an orgasm felt like.

The return of Nibbles the bunny was a type of happiness I had never known. It was a type of happiness that is exclusive to widows and other victims of trauma. I feel very smug about this, and you should, too. Had I been a normal person with a prodigal bunny, her return to me might have merely given me a sense of relief, but because I am a batshit-fucking-crazy-ass-traumatized-affair-victim widow, her return to me was equivalent to the second coming of Jesus Christ. If you were a Christian, that is. If you are not a believer in the Rapture like me, then the return of Nibbles the bunny can be compared to living on an island with Beyoncé and consuming a form of chocolate cake this has been chemically altered to be calorie free.

One of the more common questions I get in my e-mails these days is from widows asking me if they will ever be happy again. I tell them no, that they will never again know the same happiness they once had before their lives were shit on. But what they will come to know is batshit crazy joy. Because we have all been living in various stages of rage, depression, and probably inebriation every second of the night and day since the loss of our spouses, our potential for this unique type of joy is vast. Unfortunately these moments of batshit crazy joy are few and far between during the early years of our grief, but I promise you they are well worth the wait.

Chapter 53

From John's Blog: Meds and Feeling Check

March 9th, 2014 fourteen days before his suicide
Had to go to the doctor yesterday to get everything uped on meds. Now I'm on an anti depressant, an anxiety pill, had to have my sleeping pill uped, and I have to take a couple tylenol just to get out of bed because body aches so bad. I think I sleep very tense. Two packs of smokes and an 18 pack a week. This sucks!!

Surviving is all I'm doing. I'm def not living.

Main reasons this is, is because everything I do while even in good intentions, is wrong in her eyes and gives an opportunity to yell at me for a while. Great. And I'm so mad at myself that I can't do anything right. Why is that? What do I do? This is so confusing! If I don't talk I get yelled at for taking too long. If I do talk I say all the wrong things and get yelled at. This sucks.

 I guess my feeling would be as of right now:
Scared
Lonely
Afraid
Sad

Confused
Anxious
Depressed
Devastated
Did mention confused?
Happy (I have my kids this weekend)

I just wish hopeful was one that I was feeling but it's not looking that way. I keep asking god for mercy and forgiveness, but again I think he's busy right now.

Chapter 54

The Sex Buffet

The other night I happened to be in a Jacuzzi with three men and a bottle of whiskey. You know, just a typical Sunday night for yours truly. As whiskey-laced conversations often go, ours became deeper with each pour. A discussion of friends these men had lost to suicide arose, and I asked them all how their friends' widows were coping. This lead to a discussion of grief sex.

"I could never have sex with someone who had just lost their husband," said guy number one. "I'd feel too much like I was taking advantage or something."

"I would! If a widow needed sex, I'd do it," said guy number two with a tone full of sincerity and devoid of humor.

Guy number three just lit his cigarette.

Right there in front of me were the polarized opinions of the masses when it comes to grief sex. Some see sex after loss as harmful or disrespectful; some see it as helpful and natural; some people ignore the very notion of it; and then you have people like me, who see grief sex as one big food analogy.

The way I see sex after death, particularly after the death of a spouse, is like food. Some people simply can't eat while in mourning, and some people put on their stretchy pants and hit the all-you-can-eat buffet.

I hit the buffet.

The unending choices that online dating provided me with and my ability to put whoever I wanted on my plate was how I regained my sense of power back after the free fall that was my husband's suicide.

I regret none of it. Not even the guy with erectile dysfunction. The man buffet was a necessary part of my early grief.

Yes, please, I'll take another scoop of that twenty-two-year-old gym rat with extra surfer-guy gravy on the side. No, wait, put him on top, thanks.

Why, yes, I'll have a third slice of that sweet bartender and his cold-hearted ice-cream friend next to him. Extra whipped cream.

No, thank you, to the emotionally healthy salad-bar man with a savings account and kind eyes. I'll stay over in the deep-fried, fucked-up biker-guy section with the men whose engines are always running hot and their feelings for me cold.

There were very few times during my sex-buffet years when I felt taken advantage of. For the most part, grief sex was an outlet for my rage and a way to regain my sense of power during those early years while in a perpetual state of free fall.

The loss of power that comes with the loss of a spouse, particularly in cases of suicide, is something no one can prepare you for. Having my husband kill himself was to have the earth removed from under my feet. It was to fall into a void that was darker than pitch black, only to land in a deeper void that was filled with infinite voids. It was to scream at the top of my lungs with no sound coming out and no one around to notice me. It was not having power taken from me; it was the realization that I never had any to begin with.

In so many ways, his death was also my own.

Sex is the opposite of this. And while we are at it, so are all-you-can-eat buffets! The consumer gets to choose who, how, when, and how much. We cannot choose this with our spouses' deaths, which is why a lot of widows and widowers have a lot of sex soon after their spouses' funerals.

And sometimes *at* their spouses' funerals. (Had I not had my children surgically attached to me at my husband's funeral, I probably would have had sex with a groundskeeper or something!)

The loss of power is an interesting and universal part of the human experience, especially in the context of widowhood. Lack of power, and the trek to regain a sense of it, manifests in so many different ways. Some find power in prayer, some find power in food, some find power in creating a charity, some find power in exercise, some find power in traveling, some find power through art, and some find it through sex.

The only difference in these quests to regain our sense of power is how outsiders react to them. There is this undertone of expectations every culture has for how their widows are to behave; here in America, you are a good little widow if you participate in church and charity, and you are a bad little widow if you participate in beer pong and car sex.

I am a bad widow, and it heals me the same way that church and charity heal my "good" widow sisters. We are all the same underneath our coping mechanisms and metaphorical black veils. At the end of the day, as we crawl into our big, empty beds, we are all just widows. Not good or bad—just hurting, and so very beautiful.

Chapter 55

Sit

It seemed like Veronica was there every day, especially when the others had gone back to their lives, even though they had all promised me they'd be there after the funeral. She'd bring her guitar and her razor-sharp wit, and she'd just play—or not. A lot of my memories of those early days are of her sitting silently on the couch, adjacent to me. She somehow knew that the best thing to say to me was nothing. She somehow knew that words could not fix something so unjust. She gave my loss dignity by silently acknowledging that the pain was not something she would dare to understand. Sometimes she would offer me water, sometimes she would play with the kids, and all of the times she would make me feel safe.

She was sixteen years old. How did she do this? When those around her who were older and supposedly wiser say and do all the wrong things, she just knew to sit.

Chapter 56

My Diary: What If?

October 13, 2015

What if it's all been a lie? My whole life. What if I never wanted marriage, family, God, the house? What if I am someone who was supposed to be unattached? What if I only became who I thought I should be, and what if I've only ever done what I thought I was supposed to do?

I really and truly believe I will not find romantic love again. I will not grow old with a man. I will not share my life or my bed with a man. It's not what I want. It's not who I am anymore. Maybe it never was. Maybe I am enough. My kids are the best thing I ever did.

Chapter 57

Wonder Widow

I first realized I had superpowers about two months after John's death. I was out of state at a birthday party for a good friend whose other friends only knew me from a distance. The last time they had seen me was years ago with my (alive) husband and our two children at a wedding.

Word spread quickly through the party that day that I was now widowed to (gasp!) suicide, after a partygoer casually asked me, "So where's John this weekend?" and I responded with, "In an urn in his parents' living room. That's where bad husbands who shoot themselves have to go."

And gradually, as the whispers and stares began to increase (along with the vodka in my fruit punch), I felt a cold sensation ascend my body. I was morphing into Wonder Widow, and my first superpower was the cloak of invisibility. I think I even sprouted a cape…an invisible one, of course.

No one could see me once they heard I was widowed, let alone talk to me, and they liked it this way. I did not.

I proceeded to get drunk and talk to my reflection in the bathroom mirror every fifteen minutes or so for the remainder of that party. I don't remember what I said to drunk Michelle, but I do remember feeling small that entire weekend and completely inhibited by my invisibility. I wanted so badly to be normal, to have normal conversations with the Norms, but

I was no longer normal. I was Wonder Widow, able to repel humans and become invisible in two sentences or less!

As widowhood dragged on, the next superpower that was brought to my attention was flying, which wasn't nearly as graceful or cool as it sounds, because when Wonder Widow flies, she's basically just catching air as she falls from the barstool to the sticky floor.

Years went by with my superpowers overpowering me until I discovered the superpower that changed everything: my super strength.

It started slowly at first with the discovery that my ability to become invisible could be a good thing. The Norms didn't want me around? Well, good, I don't want to be around them, either! I began to use my super strength to take my power back as I dropped the widow bomb in conversations as early as possible with strangers to gauge if they were a Norm or a Cray. The Norms would thankfully make me invisible, and the Crays would laugh at my dead-husband jokes.

If I could use my widow superpowers to weed out the Norms and create bonds with the Crays, what else could I do?

I could fly. Eloquently this time.

I realized this last Tuesday, when I was flying down the Pacific Coast Highway with the windows rolled down and Courtney Love blaring on my car stereo. Courtney Love always makes me think of flying off barstools. Try as I might, though, I could not recall the last instance when I flew off a barstool. As of late, I had been too busy soaring above my drunken depression and looking down at the buildings of my past traumas that seemed so very surmountable to me now. It was 78 degrees, not a cloud in sight, and the smell of the ocean intoxicated me. As I thought to myself, *I still can't believe I get to live by the beach*, my cape not only became visible but also became covered in glitter.

On that Tuesday, I was an eloquently flying Wonder Widow on a secret Wonder Widow mission.

The mission? Gum balls. Yes, I, Wonder Widow, was following a guy around San Diego County who was selling me his gum ball machines. I really want to make a "ball" joke right now, but I won't because I am a lady.

Why was I buying some guy's gum ball machines? Because widowhood is fucking weird, that's why! Five years ago I was living in a tiny little desert town that no one has ever heard of, working a nine-to-five, with dreams of going to seminary and growing old with my husband. Now I am living in San Diego with my best friend, five kids, a dwarf bunny, and a beta fish that has ich disease, with dreams of owning five hundred gumball machines so that I never have to go back to working a nine-to-five again.

If that's not flying elegantly, then I don't know what the hell is.

Widowhood takes. It doesn't care if you are down so low that you are buried; it will kick you anyway. It doesn't care about your open wounds; it will salt them. Widowhood will take your power from you, and any power you do have, it will use it against you.

The power you once had over your emotions? Gone. The power you once had over how people perceived you? Gone. The power you once had to say no to that cocktail at 8:00 a.m.? Gone.

But once widowhood has beaten you down, broken you beyond recognition, and unmercifully buried you under twenty-five tons of shit, you will be presented with a choice. You can go deeper, stay where you're at, or put on your damn cape and fly.

Living through widowhood means that you have been forced to hold your head up high among the whispers and stares. It means you have tied your toddler's shoes while crying. Widowhood means you have felt the physical weight of his old shirt at night as you slept in it, and you still kept right on breathing. Widowhood means you have carried his burdens and yours and possibly those of your children every damn day since you heard the words, "I'm sorry, ma'am; he's gone."

Widowhood also means you have super strength. It's there whether you have tapped in to it or not. Over time, you will have muscles the size of the universe, built over sleepless nights, screams, tears, and a necessity to survive. Flex them, my little Wonder Widows! Thrive.

Chapter 58

Strip Darts

The rules to strip darts are as follows:
Objective: Orgasms

1. Strip darts must only be played on Naked Friday, while the kids are away at their grandparents' house.
2. Strip darts must be played with music. The music selection will alternate between Player 1 and Player 2's iTunes playlists.
3. No show tunes, as Player 1 has stated that they "kill the mood."
4. Cocktails can be present, but they are not required.
5. Player 2 is in charge of temperature control, as she is more sensitive to her climate.
6. The first player to throw a dart is determined by who wins the staring contest. (P1 and P2 look into each other's eyes until one of them caves and kisses the other. The one who kisses first throws darts second.)
7. Player throws three darts.
8. If Player misses dart board, he or she must remove an article of clothing.
9. If Player hits the inner circle, he or she removes an article of clothing off the opposing player's body.

10. If Player hits a bull's-eye, he or she gets to name a sexual favor to be performed.

If you get nothing else out of my books, blogs, podcasts, or social media ramblings, I need you to get this: when I was married, I was good, fun, and adventurous at sex…I think this is the second time I have mentioned this fact in this book.

I was a good wife.
I was a good wife.
I was a good wife.

I kept chanting this to myself last weekend as I stared at the dart board in our former garage. It was time to sell the house. I hadn't lived in it in years. The kids and I moved to San Diego nine months after his suicide and never looked back. We moved with such haste that as I wandered the barren house we once lived in, I kept finding things I left behind: pool toys, a broom, a stereo, and a single red dart.

A single red dart standing proudly in the center of the makeshift dart board after all this time.

I couldn't believe that the renters had never touched the dart. That means he was the last person to touch the dart. Or maybe it was me. *I miss both of those humans equally*, I thought as I pulled the dart from its position on the board.

I wandered the house four times last weekend—or was it five?—trying to figure out something. Something I couldn't identify. Did I need to cry? Did I need closure? Did I need to light everything on fire? Did I need to lie where our bed once was? I don't know.

I took the kids to the house twice. Isabelle took a picture off the wall of a werewolf she had drawn that her dad kept in the garage. She also took a picture of a zombie. Three years ago, when I read his suicide note for the third time, I remember that I had envisioned him writing it in the garage while glancing up every so often to see these pictures his daughter had made for him. Garrett wanted the intercom system. I had taken only the dart, but still I felt restless. What did I need to say good-bye?

Every particle of that house had its good memories and its bad. The meals, the happy birthday songs, the sex, the wall painting, and the dishwasher fixing. How many other women had he brought here? He only told me about one, but his computer spoke of others.

How many manicured hands had touched the counters that I cleaned?

How many high heels had walked on the floors that I had mopped?

Did they like the way my house was decorated?

Did they look at the pictures of my children on our walls?

Seven years I had spent in that house, working to make it ours. Working to make the air warm, light, and sanitary. And then he and his shotgun and his whores took my work and shit on it. They had turned the air...*my air*...into cold, darkness, and filth.

As I closed the French doors that led out to our patio and turned the lock for the last time, the blinds fell from the window and came crashing down at my feet. I reached down to retrieve them, to put them back up and make this place look presentable.

Then I changed my mind.

"I don't give a shit. I don't live here anymore," I said aloud. Garrett laughed.

Chapter 59

A Nice Man

It was a dream.

My heart was punctured by a little boy at work. Someone put a red piece of plastic in the wound to stop the bleeding. It was a man, a nice man, and he kept trying to get help for me but couldn't. There were two paramedics standing and staring, but they ignored me. It was like we were in a mall or school. I wanted to call John. He didn't answer his phone, and once it got to his voice mail, I could no longer speak from the injury. I saw Garrett with his class. He hugged me and acted normal, despite the giant piece of red plastic protruding from my chest. Then I saw Isabelle's teacher coming with her class, and I turned away so that she wouldn't see my injury.

I kept thinking, "I'm going to die. I need to tell my children something meaningful, something about how to live life," but I didn't know what to say. Then I removed the plastic, and blood started spraying everywhere. The nice man and I kept putting pressure on it until it stopped. I was feeling weak and tired and pale. I lay down.

I used to think the nice man in my dream was Jesus Christ. Now I know that it was me all along.

Chapter 60

The Brown Leather Jacket

In my third year of widowhood, I went to a thing called Camp Widow. Yes, such a thing does exist. When I got back, everyone kept asking me if I had gotten laid while I was there.

No. I did not.

Feel free to stop reading this if you feel the contents of this sexless chapter will no longer interest you. No, for the record, I did not get laid in my beautiful hotel room overlooking the San Diego Bay. I did not get laid in the bathroom, either. Or the hallways, elevators, or various bar bathrooms. Not even in the Jacuzzi.

I did, however, have a therapeutic experience equal to sex that involved a bed, a bunch of liquor, and a woman named Lauri. Do I have your attention now?

Lauri quickly became my camp BFF over a 9:00 a.m. Bloody Mary on day one of camp.

She is a newbie widow (less than a year out), and she is the first unpretentious vegan I have ever met. She's a tiny little thing, but by the way her eyebrows arch, you know that she could kill you if she wanted to—not that she'd want to, since she is as equally gentle as she is fierce. Something about her cheekbones when she smiled told me right away I could trust her, and so I did—not an easy thing for a woman such as myself, who has been widowed by her husband's years of infidelities and eventual suicide. I have a feeling Lauri has spent most of her life having her depth and her intelligence underestimated. Oh, and it has to be said that her resemblance in body language, facial features, and attitude are identical to Kit Deluca in *Pretty Woman* (minus the whole prostitute thing).

Just before the big masquerade ball on the final night of camp, I began the trek back up to my hotel room from the conference room where I had just led a workshop, so that I could change into my evening dress. Leading a workshop at Camp Widow was a great and humbling experience. The entire camp experience had been great, as a matter of fact. I couldn't believe that a large group of widows had taken time out of their lives and chosen to sign up for my workshop. Furthermore, I couldn't believe that the director of Camp Widow had entrusted me with such a responsibility knowing full well what an unsophisticated grief shit storm my social media persona is. I was overwhelmed with the faith that people had in me, and because of this, on the elevator ride up to the twelfth floor, I could feel that tears were imminent.

These days, happy occasions seem to make me cry more than sad ones.

I should've been grinning ear to ear. All weekend I had people coming up to me, screaming, crying, and asking me to sign their books…and their breasts. I had people telling me they loved me, my kids, my social media, my blog, my book, and that my humor and writing had saved them.

Yes, I should've been ecstatic, and I was—until I wasn't. I was drowning in self-doubt and guilt by the time I found myself alone in my hotel room crying until the glue from my ridiculously long false eyelashes dissolved, repeating over and over again, "I don't want to be a widow anymore. What the fuck am I doing here?"

It was around that time Lauri came to my room to escort me to the ball. There I was, crying, my false eyelashes falling down my face as I declared, "I don't want to be a widow anymore!" Lauri greeted me with hugs and high cheekbones. I busted out the mini liquor bottles.

I don't know how much time had passed or how much liquor we drank, but as the sky got dark, I found myself engulfed by a story Lauri was telling me about a brown leather jacket.

The gist of it was that years ago, she had fallen in love with a brown leather jacket that she could not afford. She would go visit it a few times a week, try it on in front of the department store mirror, and then put it back. She did this for months and looked forward to each visit. One Christmas, her husband bought the brown leather jacket for her, and she wept. She didn't have the heart to tell him that she wasn't crying tears of joy; she was crying tears of disappointment. She was crying because she would miss the hope she had when going to visit that brown leather jacket.

As I chugged the last part of my mini vodka bottle, she ended her story innocently by saying, "You know…sometimes you just have to learn to appreciate the dream that doesn't come true." That statement really got to me. She had appreciated the brown leather jacket more when she didn't have it.

No one was at Camp Widow because his or her dream had come true. All of our dreams had been mutilated, thrown out, and disintegrated while we stood helplessly on the sidelines. I realized that I had spent a lot of time focusing on the death of my dream and the death of my John instead of appreciating the fact that at one time, I did have the ability *to* dream, and I miss that. I haven't been brave enough to dream again, specifically when it comes to romantic love, but on the drive home the next day, I realized that when Lauri had found me, I was crying while sitting on a bed. Not a bathroom floor, not a carpeted floor, not lying in the bed, but sitting upright.

My next goal is to cry standing up. And then after that? Maybe I will dream of love again.

Chapter 61

I'd Rather Be Phillip's Wife Than John's Widow

I used to love a boy named Phillip. He was nineteen, and I was twenty-one. It was 2004, and we were both addicts together. He was addicted to drugs that had slang names I had never even heard of, and I was addicted to loveless sex and sexless love It was a hot month, both literally and figuratively. Summer had come early, and in the month of March, we found ourselves skinny-dipping after midnight in the pool at my apartment complex.

He would say things to me like, "Let's pretend we are in love," while we danced naked in my living room to Kenny Chesney. "Let's actually be in love," I would respond, like the good little love junkie I was. And then we would smile and do things to and with each other that I cannot write about because my kids might read this one day. In all my memories of Phillip, it was always night, and the moon was always full.

And then I met John. My future husband. My future adulterous husband. My future adulterous dead husband.

For a whole week, I loved John and Phillip both. Both wanted to marry me. Being at the top of a love triangle was the most awake I'd ever been. What's precious to me now about this time in my life is the optimism and simplicity of how we three viewed marriage. They loved me, and I loved them, so obviously marriage was the next step. No one bothered to ask anything logical like what their credit scores were, if they had any medical conditions or, you know, what their last names were. We, like most adults in their infancy, made all our decisions based on intuition, feelings, and hormones…Logic be damned!

After that one hot month and that one hot week, John told me to choose. I chose him without hesitation…Intuition, feelings, and hormones be damned! Logic had won, and Phillip had lost. I patted myself on the back for being a "real" adult. Phillip was devastated. He showed up that night at 3:00 a.m. on my doorstep, crying and telling me he loved me. Yep, Phillip was crazy; this act of passion had confirmed it. John was not crazy. He was not a drug addict. He was too rigid to skinny-dip and too practical to dance naked. John was the good choice.

Ten years almost exactly to the date that I chose John over Phillip, John would be crying and telling me he loved me as he shot himself.

I didn't immediately think of Phillip that night; I didn't immediately think of anything other than our children that night, but months later I would find myself searching Instagram for Phillip. I realize now that I wasn't searching just for him. I was searching for a piece of myself that had been lost ten years ago, another piece that had been lost when John fired that gun, and all the pieces of my younger self that I had been lost in between the ten-year gap of Phillip and widowhood.

Instagram would tell me that Phillip was now married with three daughters. All of them had his blue eyes and their mother's brown curls. It would tell me that he was sober, in love with his wife, had a stable job, and loved to barbecue. Instagram would tell me that I should've chosen Phillip.

I realize saying this makes me a bad widow and an even worse mother, but there you have it: regret. Who would I be today if I'd chosen Phillip? Certainly not this broken, anxiety-ridden, bitter, pessimistic, bitch whom everyone loves to be entertained by on social media. I would be in a kitchen somewhere in Texas, preparing side dishes to go with Phillip's barbecue, with my hope, faith, and innocence still intact.

I don't care if the person I am and the place I am at in my life is amazing right now—and yes, my life here in San Diego is amazing—I don't want it. What it has taken to get me here, to get me to be the person who lives a life so boldly with her best friend and five children by the beach, is not worth the suffering that got me here.

I'd rather be Phillip's wife, not John's widow.

But soon I won't want this. You see, it's 4:00 a.m. as I write this, and I know that this regret (like my capacity to love a man) will not last; it comes and goes as mysteriously as my joy. My kids will be up soon with their little drool-crusted faces and hair like mine, matted and unkempt. We'll fill our day up with appointments, work, and arguing over who left their cereal bowl in the sink, and in the midst of me caving in and scrubbing the damn cereal bowl myself, I will wonder how I got to be so very fortunate to have this life. Tonight Lynnette and I will have a few glasses of wine on our backyard palette couch that we built ourselves and laugh about the arbitrary things that made up our day.

I will go to bed not regretting one single choice I ever made because what John gave to me was equal to what he took from me, and I will be so content and full of wine.

Chapter 62

Things I Wrote on Facebook on His Death Anniversary

March 23, 2017

Dear John,

You've been gone for three years today, and if I believed you could hear me, I'd talk to you and tell you that you won. You set out to break me, and so you have.

This year has been the hardest. I've cried more than the first two years combined. I've hated you less and myself more.

Most days I just can't be angry with you. I miss being angry with you.

Today I can't stop thinking about how you were once a little boy. What happened to him? Did I kill him, or did you? Maybe it was just life. I see now how life kills the innocent.

My son still wears your shirt to bed every night. Every night for three years. The way it falls off his little shoulders makes him look so very young and so very old, too.

Sometimes he still refers to you in the present tense.

"Daddy loves cosmic brownies!"

"Yes, dear, Daddy *did* love cosmic brownies."

My daughter found one of your legal-pad journals last month and read it before I could stop her.

"Daddy really did have a sick brain, huh, Mom?"

"Yes, dear. He really did toward the end."

They ask harder questions now. Questions I cannot answer.

"Did Daddy go to heaven?"

"Is there such a thing as heaven?"

Still, even with all of this, there is relief. I don't feel guilty about the relief anymore. Your daily pain was a heavy burden, and it's no longer mine to carry. Maybe it should never have been, or maybe this was love. I don't know.

With sincerity,
Michelle Miller

March 23, 2016

Dear John,

And so we made a home there, the kids and I, inside the grief, because we did not have a choice. And here we are two years later.

Time does not heal. Anger does not subside, and neither does love. And despite all the things you took from us 730 days ago, we are still here, still intact, and still able to experience joy. Today I feel proud of that and proud of so many other things.

Proud of myself because I stopped apologizing for who the grief has turned me into, proud of the few people who have stuck by me because I am so very difficult to understand, and proud mostly of my babies who still dare to bond with new people even though their lives so far suggested that they would not.

I will not mourn you today; so many other days have been devoted to the act of mourning. Instead I will celebrate the resilience of me and my kids, and it will involve pancakes—lots of pancakes, because pancakes and anger are the only way to make it through days like this.

With sincerity,
Michelle Miller

March 23, 2015

Dear John,

I have been told this year that I haven't been grieving you properly. I wear makeup and cute dresses, and I (gasp!) smile. Apparently I'm supposed to be wearing a black veil the rest of my life.

Fuck that. I look better in pink.

One year ago today, you took your life, but I refuse to let you take mine and the kids'. So if grieving you with anger, laughter, and pink dresses has made me the target of others' judgments, so be it. I know better. I know I have grieved you with tears as well.

I have cried fat tears. The ones that sit in my eyes and cloud my vision before they fall, while I'm watching the slow spinning of the ceiling fan in the silence of the bedroom we once shared.

I have cried furious tears. The ones that stream from my eyes and fill the frown lines on my face, while I'm smashing your shit with a hammer.

I have cried gentle tears. The ones that leak from my eyes without warning, while I'm driving to the gas station on a random Tuesday afternoon, and our song plays on the radio.

I have cried hysterical tears. The ones that only come when it's dark, while I'm alone on the bathroom floor, begging God to take me from this earth.

I have cried for you. But not today.

Today I will not mourn you, even though I realize it would be the appropriate thing to do. As you know, I've never been very good at following the rules of propriety. And also, I'm not "there" yet. "There" in that magical land where all your sins have been erased so that I can remember you fondly like everyone else seems to do. I knew you far too well for such blind idolatry.

The only sadness I will have today is for your family and your true friends, the ones who never saw anything but the best of you.

As for my kids and I, we have had enough sad days this year, and we will surely have more to come. Grieving my kids' futures has been an especially hard pill to swallow. Future days when they are supposed to be experiencing uncomplicated joy like their weddings and graduations. Days marked with unofficial rites of passage and their new babies. Days you chose not to be a part of but will inevitably be included in through the lingering sting of your abandonment.

So today we will not mourn. We will celebrate the new life we've made for ourselves and the miracle of us not only surviving these past twelve months, but also thriving in the mess you left us.

I loved you, I hated you, and I feared you. I no longer fear you, but the other two remain.
With sincerity,
Michelle Miller

The harsh judgments and oppressive blame I've had to live with the past twelve months could have taken me under if not for the opposing forces of love and acceptance that have been poured on me and my kids. To the fiercely loyal circle of people who have surrounded my little family of three this year, I thank you.

March 23, 2014
Never again will there be any night. No one will need lamplight or sunlight. The shining of God, the Master, is all the light anyone needs. And they will rule with him age after age after age.
—Revelation 22:5 The New Living Bible

Chapter 63

Cremation Jewelry

Sometimes I miss my sanity.

My nostalgia for it usually happens when the clock in my bedroom changes from midnight to 12:01 a.m., and I am forced to accept that I am officially in the pits of insomnia. Again. It is around that time that I start thinking about Sam—you know, from *Sleepless in Seattle*? I never fully understood him or this movie until I, too, became widowed. If my widowhood were a movie, it would be called *Sleepless in San Diego*...or it would be called *Grief Sex and the City*...but that's an entirely different book altogether.

Sleeplessness. Ugh.

Insanity. Double ugh.

Grief sex. Yes, please.

Sanity. Oh, how I miss thee! I miss catching a cold and not automatically assuming I am dying of cancer. I miss filling my head with the kids' weekly schedules instead of eulogies for my friends and family. I miss the days when my biggest parenting dilemma was teaching the kids how to do their own laundry instead of teaching them how to spot the warning signs of depression and suicide, because I know now that they are genetically predisposed to this disease, and I can't unknow that.

I miss my sanity.

Garrett recently misplaced the cremation necklace he got from my in-laws a few years ago...The fact that the words "cremation necklace" are even in my vocabulary really pisses me off...I miss the days when my son asked me to spend sixty-five dollars on a Nerf gun. As a mother, you can always say no to a sixty-five-dollar Nerf gun. You cannot, however, say no to a sixty-five-dollar piece of jewelry that encases the ash of your son's father.

You just can't.

So I ordered him a replacement cremation necklace, and it arrived at our doorstep at 7:35 a.m. My son insisted that we fill it right then and there, so he could wear it to school.

I miss the mornings when my biggest problem with my son was getting his cowlick to stay down.

A cowlick is nothing compared to a small plastic funnel being clogged with what I can only assume is a bone fragment from my husband's body. After breaking two wooden toothpicks and defiling a pair of scissors with my husband's remains, I was beginning to panic. The clock was ticking, and I had to get my son out the door for school *with* a cremation necklace around his neck. I *had to*!

Only you widows with children will fully understand my drive to accomplish this task and how guilt about our kids' dead parent drives absolutely every single action, thought, and feeling every second of every day.

After ten minutes of battling with my husband's bone fragment, I had convinced myself that my son's emotional well-being depended upon me forcing that damn bone fragment into that ridiculously small tube that was feeding into an even smaller opening of a cremation-remains capsule.

I grabbed yet another toothpick. I jammed, swiveled, and pricked that stupid bone fragment with the same enthusiasm I once had for Pinterest back in my married days. As the clock inched closer and closer to the time that the school bell would be ringing, I stabbed, jabbed, and crammed that little wooden stick into that funnel with all of my widow might!

And then it happened.

I took one last giant strike into that godforsaken funnel hole and yelled out at my husband in frustration, "Stop being so damn stubborn, John!" And with that statement, the plastic funnel went one direction, and the small cross necklace went in the other. The ashes went all over my leggings. Garrett and I started laughing.

Sometimes I do not miss my sanity at all.

Chapter 64

From John's Blog: Forest Gump

March 10, 2014 thirteen days before his suicide

I had a forest gump moment today. After I said goodnight to my kids I decided to take a jog. Well I got to the end of a road and said to myself "I'm really not that tired" so I continued. And this happens a couple different roads for a while. But about half way through it became an experiment. What was going to give out first? My left knee? My right knee? My heart? My mind?

My knees have always been bad. My heart hurts every second of the day, kinda feels like I'm having a heart attack. And my mind has been mush since all of this has gone down with my soul mate, my wife.

110 min later I am near a friends house and he happened to still be up and he said I can drop by. I asked him for a ride home, which I am very appreciative of, because I was still 5 miles away from my house, and he said yes. Cool. I retraced my path with my trucks odometer and I ended up going almost 10 miles. Actually it was 9.8 but 10 sounds better.

So I did somewhere around 11 min miles for almost 2 hours. Not too bad considering I haven't ran in over a year. I drink a 2 liter a day of coke and I smoke 2 packs of smokes a day, and yes I do inhale.

So in conclusion; I'm not sure who won the experiment. My knees hurt pretty bad. Surprising though my calves are hurting pretty bad too.

I still am having heart problems. And pardon the language my mind is still f–ked up as ever.

Chapter 65

Three Things to Say to a Widow

"Well, he never believed in God, so now that he's dead, I guess he knows the truth," said the religious man. And so began the litany of awkward, insensitive, and (of course) "well-meaning" condolence comments in reference to my husband's suicide that I would have to endure, in addition to the constant vomiting and perpetual shaking of my hands for the next year.

Four days later, it would be, *"Well, I can always take you out to dinner next weekend; I clean up nice,"* as another religious man rubbed my back a little too long for my comfort level during the obligatory "hug-the-widow" show that took place at the buffet table near the entrance of the reception.

My husband shot himself. Casseroles and hugs for everyone!

"You'll remarry. You're so pretty and young!"

Because if I were ugly and old, I wouldn't get that luxury?

"I just want you to know that I don't blame you at all. It was his choice to shoot that gun."

Thanks for reminding me that everyone else does indeed blame me.

"How are you?"

Fucking fabulous, thanks.

"I'm here for you."

Except you won't be about three seconds after the funeral reception, when you return to your own life and decided that "here for you" means occasionally liking my social media posts.

"He's in a better place."

No he's not. He was an atheist who denied the existence of God up until his final breath. I heard his final breath on the phone as he shot himself; trust me, he's not in *your* version of a "better place."

"His death happened for a reason."

Yes. The reason is that when a bullet enters the body at point-blank range, it kills you.

"I know exactly how you feel. When my great-aunt Agnes died…"

Yep. That's the same thing.

"Why did he kill himself?"

While I appreciate your nosiness, I'm gonna decline that question for now and ask that you please do not speak to me again until you have adequately researched suicide and mental illness. Idiot.

"I'm praying for you."

Great! While you're at it, please make sure to tell God I no longer believe in him. Thanks.

What do all of these questions and statements have in common? None of them brought me comfort, and about half of them aggravated my already indescribable pain.

These people were not insensitive assholes (well, except maybe the first two men I mentioned); they were just uneducated about the true needs of those who are in mourning. Years and years ago, when I was a Norm, I was also guilty of using some of these cute little grief catchphrases. I am guilty, in my past life, of asking things I should never have asked and making promises to mourners that I never intended on keeping ("Call me any time of the day or night, and I will be there for you!"). I have said these phrases to children who have lost grandparents, and I have said them to grandparents who have lost siblings. Most regretful of all, though, I have said these things to widows. And then I became one at the age of thirty-one.

Now that I'm living this experience, I know better, and so I do better. Doing better to me means spreading awareness of how to help those in mourning so that they are not further injured on top of their lifelong grief. I have talked to hundreds of widows in the last few years through social media and in person, and we all mostly agree that the three things every widow/er needs you to say to them are as follows:

1. Nothing…followed by a statement about how you are not going to be saying anything. At all cost, avoid words. Never underestimate the power of shutting the hell up, especially early on. The only exception is if you want to acknowledge your commitment to silence by saying, "There really are no words for what has happened to you," or, "I don't know what to say," or, "If there were words in existence to comfort you, I would say them."
2. Nothing…followed by validation. If you are ever lucky enough to be the person a widow comes to vent, you have one job and one job only: to validate him or her. You can validate that person by listening and nodding in silence with lots of eye contact and attentive body language, or you can validate that person by saying things like, "Absolutely! This is not fair, and you have every right to be angry." Do not offer unsolicited advice. Ever. More often than not, when people come to talk to you, they are not seeking answers; they simply want to be heard and understood. Let them know that every feeling they have is being heard and that they are not crazy.
3. Nothing…followed by action. Yes, food and money in those early weeks are helpful. Do that. But also be aware that grief is a lifelong process, and helping someone who is grieving should be, too. It's a marathon, not a sprint. Two years after the funeral, deliver (or have delivered) a meal on a school night. Find out when her wedding anniversary is, and take her out for a margarita. Show up to her child's baseball game. Five years (or ten or twenty) later, randomly call on a Sunday, and see if she needs anything picked up from the store. Action.

Early on in my widowhood, I could not identify my needs. I could barely identify which shoes were mine and which shoes belonged to my seven-year-old son. I am forever grateful for the people who knew my needs and still fulfill those needs for me now, almost three years later.

Chapter 66

I Miss

I miss denial the way I miss hope, the way I miss ignorance, the way my Garrett misses the dead worm he buried when he was three years old, the way Isabelle misses her best friends from summer camp. Hope is so much a part of denial, so much a part of what kept me alive in those early weeks and months after John's sex-addiction revelations.

I miss optimism, innocence, and the willingness to see the best in people at all costs. I miss denial when I look at old pictures of John and me. I miss denial even more when I run into one of the Hos at the grocery store, and I miss denial the most when it is replaced by depression.

Chapter 67

Cocktail Recipes for Life after Your Husband's Affair

The "My Husband Likes Other Women" Margarita: Go to your local Mexican restaurant. Order a large margarita and a large to-go water with a lid and straw. Dump the water out in the bathroom, and return to your table with the empty cup. When the judgmental waitress isn't looking, put the margarita in the to-go cup, take it home, crawl back under the covers, and sip it until you fall asleep.

The "Michelle's Trying to Be Under 100 Pounds So Her Husband Will Love Her Again" Low-Calorie Vodka Float: three shots of whipped-cream vodka, one can of diet vanilla root beer, one scoop of no-sugar-added vanilla bean ice cream.

The "Michelle Needs Caffeine Because the Nightmares of Her Husband Having Sex with Everyone Have Kept Her Awake for 48 Hours" Rum and Coke "Di-cardi": three shots of Bacardi, one can of Diet Coke.

Chapter 68

They'll Wind Up at Harvard One Day

On a Monday, I got notes from both my kids' teachers that informed me they were getting the Student of the Month Awards that month, and so I went to the kids' school for the monthly awards assembly. No makeup, hair in a ponytail, baggy jeans, and a hoodie. As I watched my offspring get their certificates of accomplishment, I tried to pass off my tears as ones of pride and joy instead of guilt and defeat. I began to think, "This is great! Even though I haven't been around much, my kids are doing well. That means I have raised smart, independent children! Good job, Michelle!" Swiftly, depression reminded me that my kids would be better off without me. After I took pictures of their proud little faces framed by their awards, the truth hit me. They are doing better in school now that I stopped helping them with their homework and spending time with them, because I am a bad mother. Maybe if stayed out of their lives completely, they'd wind up at Harvard one day.

Depression is an asshole. I missbeing in denial.

Chapter 69

I Just Knew

In the nearly ten years since I've known him, John had never physically harmed me, until that freezing January night in 2014. The slow, downward spiral he had taken physically and mentally the past two and a half years since his secret life was exposed had been severe and excruciating for me to watch. To say he was a shell of a human being downplayed his hollowness. He was dead in every way possible except for the physical.

He chain-smoked Swisher Sweets Cigars; called off work at least once a week; slept only four hours a night in our unfinished garage that he had chosen to move into; became obsessed with prepping our home and cars for end-of-the-world scenarios; stopped shaving and getting haircuts; obsessively cleaned his gun collection; quit counseling and Sexaholics Anonymous; and survived on a diet of microwavable pizzas, Little Debbie Snack cakes, and a two-liter bottle of Pepsi every single day.

He lived in a constant state of anxiety and paranoia, and he channeled his nervous energy into reading everything on the Internet about how to survive the end of the world and micromanaging my life. It was a horrible existence for us both. He chose the clothes I wore each day (modest), the food I ate (high in calories), the places I went (work, the grocery store with him, or out to eat with friends if I was home in under an hour), and the makeup I wore (no false eyelashes and no lipstick). I would sneak out to go to the gym and the beauty salon, but I couldn't enjoy them because I was so afraid of getting caught. If I didn't text him constantly when I was out of his sight, he'd show up at my work or on outings with my friends "just to say hi."

The absurdity of his doing these things when *he* was the one who was unfaithful still baffles me. I was incarcerated for a crime I didn't commit. I could have lived like this forever; some people do. Eventually all prisoners stop yearning for freedom.

Making up excuses for his odd behavior and my high-collared necklines paired with baggy jeans was getting more difficult and increasingly embarrassing. I convinced myself to endure this behavior because "at least he was still a good father"…when he was around, anyway, and I really believed this obsession-with-me phase would blow over, not get worse.

I begged him to go back to counseling or try anxiety medication or a healthy diet and exercise regimen. I suggested he go out with his friends (even the ones who aided him in his affairs, because I was so desperate for him to leave me the fuck alone) or take up a hobby away from the house. He refused. I was his counselor. I was his medication. I was his food. I was his friend. I was his hobby.

I allowed this because I was exhausted from fighting, guilt ridden about taking the kids out of a two-parent household, worried about money, and sedated by antidepressants. Not to mention John's successful manipulative tactics. Although an atheist, he had somehow managed to memorize every Bible verse pertaining to wifely submission and would repeat them to me when I suggested wearing above-the-knee shorts.

He somehow missed all the verses about adultery.

This feeling of being caged was what led me to draw the line at Kate that night, which provoked John to get physical. Actually, my period and I drew the line at Kate, ironically, since Kate and I had once made a pact to never make a decision the week before or during our periods. I have come to since recognize that some of the best things in my life I've ever said, done, eaten, and purchased have been under the influence of my monthly egg release and subsequent burrowing of said egg into my uterine lining.

But I digress.

John had kept me from visiting Kate, one of my oldest and closest friends, for more than a year, and I was dying to see her soon, since she had given birth to her first baby eight months ago. Kate was, and still is, a rock. A glittered one that always shined for me. Before I found out about John's affairs, Kate and I would usually see each other three times a year by plane or car, and John never minded. Then once his affairs came to light, he had kept me from her. She never made me feel guilty about any of it. Not even when I had to miss her thirtieth birthday party. She still encouraged me to work things out with John and called daily in the early days following his affairs. But she didn't stop there. For years, she never missed a birthday card, holiday present, or weekly phone call, even when I was three weeks late sending her a birthday card and sent her phone calls to voice mail six times in a row.

That cold January night, when John got home from work, I showed him my plane ticket to Arizona. He glared at me and told me that if I went, he'd have divorce paperwork waiting for me when I got back. I told him I'd buy a souvenir pen from Arizona to sign it with. My sharp, uncharacteristic, and defiant comment shocked us both.

I love my period.

We stood there facing each other, he with crossed arms and I with my hands on my hips as a visual declaration of my war on his tyranny. My silence and hand placement spoke volumes.

I *will* wear shorts in the summer or in the winter, because they are *my* legs. I *will* eat steamed vegetables when I feel bloated because it is *my* stomach, and I *will* wear hooker-red lipstick and mile-long false eyelashes because it is *my* face. My body *was* his, it did belong to him, and his body was mine. It belonged to me when we had joined our lives together and made vows of fidelity. He broke those vows and, in turn, broke both of our claims to each other's physical being.

Likewise, he also broke the emotional relationship we had with each other, which led me to rightfully seek intimate connections with others—no, not sexual relationships, but intimate ones with my friends.

When you are single, your friends are your family. They fulfill the human desires we all have for intimate connections. When you get married, you forfeit that connection to a certain extent, and your friendships have to be second to your spouse. When your spouse abandons you, physically or emotionally, it is only natural that you gravitate back to your friends to seek out the connection that was once demoted.

Had John apologized and tried to restore his physical and emotional connection with me the last few years, things would have been different. But he had not, so they weren't. We were irreparably broken due to the lack of repair on his part and passage of time, and my friendships would not suffer the same fate.

Humans need connection. A connection he denied me when he was unfaithful and was now was trying to deny me of having with my friends.

I will visit my friends whenever I want without checking in with John every thirty-six seconds, I will travel to nurture my friendship if need be, I will fight for Kate, and when I get back from seeing her, I will fight for monthly visits to San Diego to see Lynnette.

After what seemed like an eternity of my unwavering hand-on-my-hip placement in the silence of our bedroom, John snapped.

As I lay in bed later that night after he fell asleep, rubbing the sore he had left on my chest, I couldn't stop smiling. I knew I would not do this anymore. John had given me the out I needed. I would not subject my children to the increasingly dangerous life this incident had opened the doors to. I knew then that leaving him for good was an act of mercy for our whole family. I didn't want him to be this violent, controlling person anymore; I wanted better for him. I didn't want my children to develop into adults under a roof of uncertainty and tension. I wanted better for them. I didn't want to be this fearful, medicated victim; I wanted better for me.

I wanted a lot of things that I would never have: a slice of cake at my fifty-year wedding anniversary, an apology from him, an apology from all the Hers, a traditional family for my kids, and a chance to relive my twenties. I knew these things were no longer possibilities for my future. No, they would not be a part of my life, but a divorce from John, a divorce from the oppressive life he was trying to force me into, and freedom from the burden of trying to "forgive" him and heal our marriage, I would have, and I would have it now.

As far as I was concerned, we were already divorced and had been for years. I was free; the paperwork would be a formality.

Watching him sleep soundly, completely unremorseful about the physical damage he had just done to me, I felt accomplished. I had done absolutely everything within my power to save a marriage that was built on John's lies and my naiveté. I was no longer ashamed to walk away; I was proud. I knew that leaving behind this hopeless marriage would give me self-respect and peace. I knew it would give me the ability to salvage the parts of myself nearly obliterated by John. I knew that I gave this man all of me, and now I would take it back, because it was mine to take, and most importantly, I knew—I really and truly knew in the depths of my soul—that if I had to witness one more of John's baby-ass bitch fits about my wearing lipstick, I'd go to jail for murder and not even regret it.

I.

Just.

Knew.

If I knew then that my leaving him was going to lead to his suicide, I would have stayed. I'm glad I hadn't known this, and I'm done feeling guilty about that.

Chapter 70

Mashed Potatoes

And then suddenly we are there at his funeral, the kids and I sitting in the front pew of the church I grew up in, steps away from John's urn. I don't know how we got there, if we drove or not. I don't know if we ate breakfast or how our clothes got onto our bodies.

I glance at my dad, who's sitting at the end of the row, separated from the kids and I by eight feet of flowers and cards people had brought over to me before the service. My dad is with my mother and brother, and as I look at him, I recall him saying to me last night, "How do you plan on speaking at the funeral?"

"What do you mean?" I had asked. "I plan on getting up there and reading from the paper I wrote."

"No," he'd said gently. "How are you going to be able to do that? I just think it's going to be more difficult than you think." He was not underestimating me or patronizing me, but he was concerned he'd have to scrape me off the floor again like he'd done six days ago, when John was pronounced dead. "For me," he had continued, "I've decided to go into this thing mad, so I can get through my speech. That's my stance. I'm just mad," he declared.

So I'm mad, too. And the madness had kept my tears at bay so far today.

I didn't cry while helping Garrett set up the posters of John he'd made in the entryway of the church. I didn't cry while carrying around the entourage of stuffed animals and blankets Isabelle needed to combat her random bouts of shakes and chills. And I didn't cry when people came up to greet me, even though every face I saw—every voice I heard that day—was a reminder that I was a murderer. I had killed that person's friend, nephew, cousin, coworker, grandson, brother, uncle, and child. I did not want to talk to them. I did not want to hug them. I did not want to hear their fond memories of John.

If I would have stayed with John, there would be no funeral. There is no way around that fact. I am the cause of his death, and everyone in the sanctuary today knows it. All eyes and thoughts are on me.

Guilt is very self-indulgent.

I had decided on anger last night, which came easily to me, since hours earlier I had discovered a few of John's Hos had sent in pictures of them and John for the slide show at his memorial service. Feel free to take a moment to reread that last sentence.

Yes, anger—my old faithful friend—would get me through this day. I knew I could not cry. If one tear fell, they would all fall along with me to the ground on that horrible, outdated, turquoise carpet of my childhood church. The tears I would cry at John's funeral would not be the refined tears of an elderly widow behind a black veil who had seen her husband though a long-suffering illness and had the satisfaction of knowing she and her husband had shared a long, good life together. No. My tears, if they fell, would not be dignified. They'd be violent and would send me into hysterical convulsions with no end. My children need me, and they need me intact. I don't get to cry. Everyone else at the funeral that day gets this right, especially my kids.

Later I will discover that people took my lack of tears as evidence of my delight in John's death and my avoidance of conversation with them as a personal attack, because yeah, the day of my husband's funeral is about *them*.

Memories of the services are blurry. I don't remember the sermon, the eulogy, or the stories my dad shared about his surrogate son, John. I cannot recall standing in front of the church and giving my speech of gratitude to everyone who donated money. I felt sedated by my intense concentration to withhold my tears and stoic due to my acute awareness of everyone's fingers pointed at me. My only conscious memory of that day is the slight relief I felt when Lynnette and Kate arrived and the intensity of watching the slide show.

The slide show begins, showing John as a baby, toddler, child, and then a teen. Those pictures belonged to his family. I do not recognize that boy. I can't know him like they do: his innocence, his love of Legos, and his little face all covered with dirt.

But the pictures of him as a man are mine. They belong to me and me only, because I was his wife, and the little I knew of him, the little he chose to share with me for ten years that didn't happen to be a lie, I owned. I knew every story behind every picture. The picture of the day Garrett was born, when he left me alone after the birth for twelve hours so that he could go see Ho3. The pictures of us on Easter, when he faked a smile and told me if everyone wasn't gone by noon, he'd never forgive me. The pictures of us camping, when he left early to get a good signal so that he could watch porn.

At this point in my life, I have no good memories of John. Everyone else in that church does, but I, his bride, do not.

The trembling begins with a picture of him and me standing in front of the armoire at our first apartment. I'd find out years after this picture was taken that he'd been deep into his sexting relationship with Ho3 at the time. This was a photo his mother took of us on Father's Day.

Father's Day.

A day that will now hold an entirely different meaning for my kids.

My kids.

I have Garrett and Isabelle on either side of me in the front row of the church with my arms around them, and I pull my hands off their shoulders when the shaking reaches my fingertips. That's when the montage of photos of John and the kids begin.

My babies no longer have a father, and it's all my fault.

I look down at my lap and feel myself leaning forward. I see black spots and know I am going to faint, seize, or both. The shaking is in no way controllable. I try to will the fogginess out of my brain. I try to clarify the faded tone of the live acoustic guitars being played by my cousins. I try to talk myself out of fainting, but I know I can't, because this is not just John's life flashing before my eyes. This is *my* life and the lives of my children flashing before my eyes in three-second increments. Every three seconds, a new picture reminds me that everything I'd built our lives around had been a lie, and now that merciful lie was over.

Just as my vision goes black, I suddenly feel Lynnette's hand grasp mine. I don't know how she got there. She was sitting several pews behind me. In a split-second motion, she was there, sitting on my left, with her right arm around the kids and me, pulling us close to her while using the fingers of her left hand to interlace with the shaky fingers of my left hand and keep me off the floor.

In her embrace, both of the kids finally feel safe enough to cry. They both sob hysterically; she and I do not. I squeeze Lynnette's hand tighter and tighter until I am sure that blood will shoot from under her fingernails like laser beams. I am gasping for air as the shaking increases. We look forward, she and I, facing the slide show of my former life, our jaws clenched, our bodies rigid. She knows she cannot take away my shaking, my guilt, and my hopelessness. She knows she cannot take away the kids' tears. She just sits and supports my physical being and in turn, supports my emotional being as well. Because of her, and only her, I make it through the slide show without being hospitalized.

Lynnette, the kids, and I only stay for about twenty minutes of the reception; the guilt of seeing everyone's suffering wouldn't allow me a second more. She takes us to my parents' house and spoon-feeds me mashed potatoes and mixes martinis. The kids begin their battle to be seen as "normal" by their peers while playing in the backyard with the neighbors.

"I can't believe I just lived through that," I say in between spoonfuls of mashed potatoes.

"Me neither," she says, and she lets one tear fall down her left cheek. She's never shed a tear about John since.

Chapter 71

Hope

We buried a portion of John's ashes a few months after his funeral. I surprised myself with my willingness to experience the depression when I got home from the small ceremony. I've been so afraid to go "there" since John's death. I've been so fearful that if I had a sad day, it'd turn into sad months, and before I knew it, the kids would be neglected, the house would stop getting cleaned, and I'd be grossly underweight and attached to a heart monitor again like I had been during the affair years.

I spend the rest of the day in bed. No shower, no change of clothes.

The next morning, I get out of bed easily. The anger and guilt are back, of course, but muted. I thought for sure yesterday was the beginnings of a major depressive episode, the beginning of my true mourning for John's death. Why was my depression so short-lived?

Then I had a thought. My mourning for John had been going on for years. The man I knew and loved had died years ago. While everyone around me was just entering their grief, I had already experienced every stage several times and had developed coping mechanisms for each one. The worst of my depression was over long before he'd even written his suicide note, and this thought gave me hope.

Chapter 72

When I Started to Slowly Stop Hating God

When the last bell rang on the last day of my senior year of high school, I was elated. Free. I knew I'd never go to a university like all my friends were doing. I knew the horrible agony of going to school for the last thirteen years of my life was over, never to be revisited again. Quitting church felt a lot like that.

I never really quit God, but I definitely relieved myself from the obligation that was the four walls of a building filled mostly with ignorance, arrogance, and general good intentions. I felt relief after the initial guilt and only went to Bible study when I felt like it, as I had always preferred the small-group educational setting to the large, impersonal confines of an auditorium. Then, eventually, I stopped going to the small group. I stopped watching online sermons, stopped praying, and stopped reading my Bible altogether, and that's when I started to slowly stop hating God.

Even in my hatred and dismissal for him and of him, I'd still feel his presence every so often. Watching the kids sleep at night or listening to *The Lion King* on Broadway soundtrack, when I was having a particularly good hair day, or when I actually had a peaceful night's sleep. And sometimes I would not feel God at all. Sometimes I'd be cold and sure that there is no such thing as any sort of higher power, and we are all meaningless specks in an infinite universe, whatever the hell that means.

Sometimes, when I decided to deny his existence, things would happen. Things that were too much to be a coincidence but too little to be classified as evidence. The times I did experience something spiritual, it was always sincere and real and unmistakable. It never felt made-up or manipulative like it had in church. I would go weeks and months without ever acknowledging God, and then I'd spend days in a row mentally yelling the f-word at him, followed by ignoring him altogether. I'm pretty sure he was OK with all this, though, because I never got struck down with a lightning bolt or anything. As a matter of fact, my life just kept getting better.

Chapter 73

Candy, Wine Bottles, Erections

The drag queens are mesmerizing: the way they move, the perfected arches of their eyebrows, the colors of their lips, the glitter, the confidence, the mystery of where they hide their genitalia. I am in Nashville, Tennessee, in the middle of a semicircle of people I've only known for thirty-six hours. Well, that's not exactly true. We all "met" on Facebook years ago, and for whatever reason, these people think I'm amazing. A testament to how convincing my larger-than-life social media persona really is. I am so afraid they will soon learn the truth about me: that I am boring, depressed, and introverted. For now, though, they think I am funny and strong and interesting and worthy of being greeted at the airport with a large, pink, decorated sign. (Everyone should experience this type of airport welcome at least once in his or her life.)

I'm not sure why I'm here. Not "here" as in the drag show, but here as in Nashville, Tennessee. It's more than just the kids being at summer camp, and me needing something to do. It's more than a vacation, and it's more than just meeting people I've had fun making dick-pic jokes with on social media. I can't identify it yet, but I'm here for something, and I know it has to do with John. You see, I am not just surrounded by new friends right now. I am surrounded by John's family: his half sisters and their friends. The sisters he never met, the sisters he always wanted to know and now never will.

Bastard. I hate him for this. I spent the day before my trip to Nashville on the bathroom floor, crying over him. Crying about how we were supposed to take this trip together, crying in fear that his sisters would all be mad at me for not taking the gun out of his hands, fear that the guilt I have about this will sever the relationships I hope to have with them like it has with his family in California.

It was clear within the first few minutes of meeting each one of John's sisters—Fiona; Nellie; and poor, sober, pregnant Ruby—that this would not be the case. Although they are much younger than me, upon meeting them face to face, they make me feel protected. Like they are unapologetically on my side, even if they don't like my side or even know my side. Like they would kill anyone who even raised an eyebrow at me. They are like Lynnette and Kate, only in gang form. They also have Southern accents, which I believe to be even more terrifying.

They lavish me with gifts, they listen with enthusiasm as I tell them about the guy I dated who asked me to put my fingers in his ass, they laugh wholeheartedly when I am sending pictures of my boobs out to men on dating sites (I was in the "naked picture" stage of my grief at that time, which is a real stage—look it up), and they don't scold me when I can't control my cursing around my impressionable young niece (Auntie Shell still feels badly about this). They give me the freedom to do and say and be, and this, I believe, is the best thing anyone can do for someone who is in mourning.

Over the next week, they will parade me all around their quaint little suburban town, knocking on the doors of their friends and announcing me like I'm the queen of everything. Their friends become my friends, as Samantha, the matriarch of their girl group, pulls me to her bosom in a motherly embrace and then shows me to the kitchen. And sweet, nurturing Jackie will cover me with a blanket when I am hungover on her couch and shoo her dogs away when they try to wake me.

As the drag queen's rendition of Whitney Houston's "I Want to Dance With Somebody" is at its peak, we do just that. We dance (after a fourth

Vodka Soup for the Widowed Soul

visit to our new best friend, the bartender, of course). We dance until our feet hurt, and we dance until Nellie loses her phone, and we dance until the lights blur with the flow of our formally styled hair. We dance like we are sisters, we dance like we are free of pain, and we dance like we are drunk. Let's face it, we are hammered.

We wake up the next morning on the floors and couches of a townhouse, trying to recall the details of that night. I don't attempt to recall any, because first of all, my head fucking hurts, and more importantly, the only important thing I want to recall from last night is the lingering feeling of unconditional love and acceptance given to me by these girls.

While lying on the carpeted floor of a guest room, facing the wall, with my back to Nellie and among random pieces of cat hair and the residual smell of tequila, I hear her stirring. I hold still so I won't wake her. She wakes anyway, rolls over, and puts her arm around me. I think to myself, *I was never meant to stay married to John. He was never meant to be my family, but these girls were, and after all he put me through, his sisters are a part of the reasons I don't regret my choice to marry him.*

Over the course of the week, not only will I continue to be absorbed into this wonderful group of women, but I will also watch John's sisters struggle with his death as I take notice of the ripples of his suicide killing parts of their hope. How could he, their half brother who lived such a charmed childhood—a childhood that was so very opposite of their own upbringing—end his life? If he couldn't make it in this world with all the advantages given to him, how will they?

I try to imagine what this is like for them, but I know I am nowhere close. I wish I had more good stories about him to share with them, but I just don't. I'm not even sure if the few good memories I have of their brother are even true or genuine as I replay the words, *I never loved you, Michelle. All these years I was just playing house*, in my head, words that invalidated our past together. I want to give them hope, but I don't want it to be false. I choose my words carefully when they ask me things about John, and I try to present the facts without the edge of hatred in my voice.

I don't know if I help them in any way, but I try, knowing that in no way will I ever be able to make them feel as comforted as they have made me.

I am fascinated by everyone and observe the girls closely for the remainder of my visit. In my observations, what they all teach me about grief is a lot. Every one of the girls in this group is so beautifully broken in some way, like ceramic vases that have been smashed by a truck and then glued back together by a child. They are like the mosaic tiles that lined palaces of the ancient world. They are like how sometimes, when I wake up from a drinking binge with my makeup smeared and my false eyelash glued to my cheek, I look at myself in the mirror and admire how I am like a flawless but flawed Picasso painting. They teach me that I was naïve to try to fight the grief for as long as I had. They teach me that fear is why I tried to "fix" myself for so long. They teach me to let go. And they teach me all this without using words.

For them, I want to go back in time and remove all their traumas and deaths and the unimaginable disappointments they've all been subjected to. But for me, I want to keep them all the way they are: broken and able to see things in this life that others, who have not allowed grief to change them, cannot see, and so I decide to let the grief change me after this. I decide to let it harden me, and it was freedom. It didn't feel like freedom; it just *was* freedom.

Why was I so resistant to letting the grief overtake me? Why was I so afraid of being hardened all these years? Lots of great things in this life are hard. Candy, wine bottles, erections, and now me. I can go on dates now and have men tell me they don't like me and think, *There must be something wrong with them.* I can get attacked on my social media, called everything from a bad mother to a man-hating slut, and just laugh it off with Lynnette. I can have other drivers honk and flip me off because I suck at driving, and I don't start shaking and crying like I once did. I owe all of this to hardness, which I have channeled into strength and confidence. And I learned this from my Southern sisters, who molded their own grief into strength years ago, while still maintaining a fragility about themselves.

Vodka Soup for the Widowed Soul

When I get back to California and look at all the pictures from my trip, I cannot find one in which I look bad. I'm not saying this to be conceited. I'm saying this because every picture you take in life, when looked at with honesty, tells a story of a moment. In each of those moments, my skin is smooth, my hair falls in just the right place, and everything about my demeanor is smiling, even the pictures in which I am hungover.

I realize that I don't have back all the things that were taken from me. I still don't have hope, optimism, or innocence, but I somehow I have faith.

Chapter 74

Hair Dye

Dearest eighteen-year-old Michelle,
When that one guy at that one rave tells you to inhale something from a pipe because "it's only a little bit of pot," don't smoke it. Or smoke it, but know that it is most definitely not just "a little bit of pot."

Don't go in the portable toilet on your right; go to the one on your left. You cannot unsee the things you will see in the portable toilet on your right.

Do not ever step foot in a church again, except when you are forced to on your son's fourth-grade mission field trip. He will really love that you are there. The four walls of a church are not for you. You are not like them. You are not large and spacious and painted a particular shade of eggshell. You are white-hot, flaming pink. Your church is in theaters, concert arenas, books, bars, art museums, road trips, and salad bars and slices of pizza and salad bars with your girlfriends.

Cussing does not make you sound unintelligent. It makes you sound cool. Don't wait until you are in your thirties to start cussing.

That thing in the pit of your stomach that tells you to chase men stems from manipulation and fear, not your desire for marriage. You do not want to be married; you want to be validated and your guilt about premarital sex to be alleviated. Stop feeling guilty about premarital sex. God will get over it, and so will your parents.

Do not raise your daughter to be sweet, nice, and polite. She does not live in a sweet, nice, and polite world. She lives in Southern California. Prepare her accordingly.

Dale Earnhardt will die soon, and on that day, you will witness two subsequent deaths. One will be of a motorcycle rider whose obituary you will paper-clip into your journal and read from time to time even in your thirties, and the other death will be that thing inside yourself that always thought you were immortal. You are not immortal, and neither was that boy on the motorcycle, and neither was Dale Earnhardt, even though your dad really believed him to be.

Have your babies, because you were always meant to be a mother. Even when you are searching the yellow pages for adoption agencies and abortion clinics because you think you will be unfit, you are meant to be a mother, but you were never meant to be a wife, so don't be. You are bad at sharing space and intimacies and too controlling and too passive and too smothering to really accept a man for whom he is. You cannot change this about yourself, so accept it right now.

You won't accept this right now because you are stubborn and arrogant, so accept these faults about yourself while you are staring at your second set of divorce paperwork, Precious One. And also accept right then and there, before you even skim the stack of papers in front of you with words like "irreconcilable" and "assets" on them, that loving and marrying a man is not a requirement for a successful life, and even if it were, you still shouldn't do it, because a wife is not who you are.

So tolerate men, enjoy them during the brief time it takes them to go from mysterious to obnoxious, and then set them free. As toxic as they are to you, you are ten times more toxic to them.

Both of your estranged husbands will attempt suicide and blame you for it. One of them will complete suicide. You will not survive this, but try to survive it anyway, because your attempts will be cute, and they will create good stories for you to share with fellow grievers about what not to do.

Let your grief engulf you; it's a good thing.

Cultivate relationships with both your husband's siblings. Their siblings will be there long after these men are gone. Their influence over you will be so great that it will trickle down into your children, and in this way, the good parts of your children's fathers will become a part of them.

There are good parts about your children's fathers.

Keep the nose ring that you will get next year in your nose. When it falls out while you are having sex in a teepee in the forest, stop, and put it back in. Your nose ring is worth more than that uncircumcised man. You will want to have your nose pierced when you are in your thirties, but you will not be nearly as audacious as you were when you were nineteen, so keep the piercing penetrated by that small, silver stud.

Please.

Do not even attempt community college. It is a waste of your time and money. You will learn nothing, absolutely nothing. What motivates you to go to community college is your obsession with doing the "right" thing: the thing that would make others happy, the thing that is supposed to guarantee your success. The definition of success is not one size fits all, like that headband you shared with that girl in preschool who gave you head lice. There are no right or wrong choices, only decisions that lead us down different paths we either regret or we don't. When you finally let go of what is "right," you will have what is left, and that is better.

You will go to a palm reader later on this year, and everything that she tells you will happen will indeed happen. And this will give you peace, even though you've been taught your whole life that such practices are evil.

You will soon discover a thing called social media. You will love it and so will almost everyone else on planet earth. It will change the social structure of the planet as you know it. It will open you up to new friends you would not have met otherwise. Then there will be a movement created by very bored people to convince everyone that social media is bad and addictive. You and you alone determine what is bad for you and what has or has not become an addiction.

You won't get addicted to nicotine, so don't feel guilty about smoking cigarettes. You will, however, get addicted to the social aspect of inhaling and exhaling those cool little puffs of smoke with others who also enjoy inhaling and exhaling those cool little puffs of smoke, but you will find it easy to quit this habit because you are introverted.

Your soul mate does not have a penis.

Slather your face with sunscreen, and cover it with a towel before entering a tanning booth. Every. Single. Time.

Stop believing only the good things about humans. Humans are deeply selfish. You are a human. And so are all the people you will love and hate. Placing humans on pedestals is something naïve humans do. Don't be a naïve human.

The "friends with benefits" relationship you are currently in will never benefit you in any way and neither will any of the ones that follow.

When you are feeling lonely and invalidated, stay home, and give yourself a pep talk and ice cream. If that doesn't work, give yourself an orgasm. Your self-inflicted orgasms will be better than the ones you will get from a man—except for that one man.

Do him.

You will hate the God you currently love so much. You will tell him to fuck off and ignore him for years. Your life will improve because of your sincerity and his love and because of the realization that God as you knew him was only a creation of your imagination, self-importance, and some very arrogant Sunday school teachers. One day you will get to know the real him and realize you only got to see this because you finally let him see the real you, and the real you gives the finger to mythical beings at one o'clock on a Wednesday morning in her driveway.

When you find out that you got cheated on, tell everyone. Immediately.

Post it on social media.

Put a banner on Main Street with pictures of the other women.

Airing your dirty laundry in public is healthy and necessary for your healing.

Plus, it is funny as hell.

Get the fuck out of this small town. It is good and beneficial for some people. You are not those people, and neither are your children. All three of you need to be by the ocean. Water is therapeutic, even if all you ever do is watch it.

Don't feel guilty about not flossing; only high-strung people with crippling anxiety disorders floss daily. You are not high strung. Your anxiety is manageable, and you are the freest person you will ever know besides Lena Dunham. Lena seems pretty fucking free to me. You do not know who this is yet, but one day, you will.

Don't kiss that boy two days after your wisdom teeth get pulled. You will develop mono, and it will suck ass.

Your breasts are unusually beautiful. Women get implants to make their breasts look like yours do naturally right at this very moment on your eighteenth birthday. They will be lopsided in a few years by pregnancy and breastfeeding, so take lots and lots of photographs of them now. Walk around topless any chance you get. Show them to boys and lesbians and women with ugly breasts because they will appreciate them in a way no one else can.

You will not beat porn. It is too massive, too addictive, and too evil. You will submit to the inevitability that the type of men you love prefer it to you. You will be exhausted from this battle, so do not fight it; you will have bigger wars to lose.

Drink cocktails when your children are infants and toddlers. Not a lot, but enough to make you less rigid about bedtime and manners and more willing to dance with them to the *Elmocize* DVD that never seems to end. Dance to that hellish *Elmocize* DVD. The kitchen does not need to be cleaned right now, but your children need to see you dance to Elmocize right fucking now. You will fuck up your children like your parents fucked you up and their parents before them fucked them up. Parents fucking up children is as inevitable as you failing at diet and exercise programs.

You will fail at diet and exercise programs.

You will never love and accept your body because you live in a world that tells you not to, and you are not stronger than this world, nor are you stronger than your inclinations to be fascinated by all the toxic standards of beauty in it. But diet anyway, little love, and then binge eat, and vomit and starve, and then realize— even when you hit ninety-seven pounds—you still don't like the way you look because big butts came back into style, and you dieted yours away. Then order a pizza, but pair it with a Diet Coke, because, well, calories.

You will recall every last one of your mistakes as a parent and only a fraction of your triumphs and be perplexed as to why your children turned out to be just fine. They turned out to be just fine because, even though they did not see you dance to *Elmocize*, and you couldn't afford organic food or violin lessons, you danced with them at your sister-in-law's wedding, let them help you cook boxed mac and cheese, and taught them how to use pots and pans as drums. They also turned out just fine because even though they have half the DNA of their self-destructive father in them, they also have half the DNA of their funny mother in them, and humor usurps all kinds of unfortunate genetic predispositions.

Your parents didn't fuck you up nearly as bad as they thought they did, and your grandparents didn't fuck up your parents nearly as bad as they thought they did, and your grandparents' parents didn't, either.

Everyone is just fine.

Your children will be fine.

Even without fathers and new cars, they will be just fine.

Don't take life and the people in yours so seriously. Laugh at all of it. Make sex jokes in front of elderly people. It is not disrespectful. Make widow jokes at your husband's funeral when people feel the need to ask you if you are getting any insurance money since your husband's death was ruled a suicide. Specifically make those people uncomfortable with your widow humor.

Take the epidural with the first baby, but not with your second. Your vagina will not tear at all like it did with your first, so the pain will be manageable. Not experiencing natural birth is something you will always wonder about. You will wonder if you've missed out on an important part of your femininity. You will wonder what insights you could have gained by not underestimating the strength of your mind and your body. You will constantly underestimate the strength of your mind and body. Don't do that.

When you go to Rite Aid during the summer of your nineteenth birthday, purchase two bottles of tequila instead of one bottle of tequila and one bottle of hair bleach; your scalp will not recover from this.

Your hair will start to go gray in two years, so run your fingers through it. Inhale it. Rub the ends of it on your lips. Spend hours searching for split ends and hairstyles that make your face look thin. Close your eyes when your hairdresser massages your scalp with her banana-scented shampoos and magical fingers. Teach the boys you kiss how to run their fingers through it in a way that gives you comfort and goose bumps. Teach the boys you kiss how to care for you.

Really fall in love with your hair, even though you are mad at it for being partially wavy and 100 percent frizzy and so very not blond. Love it because it is a part of what connects you to your Sicilian grandmother, who will be gone suddenly and soon, before you have the chance to ask her all the things grandchildren should ask their grandparents. On the day your son is born, you will cry about her absence as you are braiding your hair.

Yes, love your hair, because your other grandmother is about to lose her battle with cancer, and she will take her last breaths with scraps of gray peach fuzz under a silk floral scarf, and you will feel guilty about the envy she once expressed to you over your hair as you and your mother watched the remains of her gray strands fall onto her lap when she ran her fingers through it.

So many people in your life envy your hair.

Be smug about this.

Know that the thick mass of unruly frizz that cascades down your back cannot be contained by mere hair bands and that this is a metaphor for your life and who you are in the quiet moments and in the loud moments, too. You cannot be contained by anything as fickle as hair bands and nine-to-five jobs and amorous love.

And finally, my love, purchase hair dye in bulk because even though I want you to love your hair just as it is, I also want you to look and feel young because you never let yourself look and feel young even when you were so. And hair dye might be the closest you will ever get to reclaiming your innocence, a thing that you will learn cannot be reclaimed once it is gone.

With deep love and admiration,

Thirty-four-year-old Michelle

Chapter 75

From John's Final Blog: One Good Day

March 18, 2014 Five Days before his suicide
Finally after two months of hell I had one good day.

I was looking forward to hanging out with some friends. It was great. I spent too much money but really what is money but green cotton. Met some really nice people. I stepped out of my normal comfort zone. I never buy clothes and I bought some. Weird. Lol. But also I got some shirts for my kids. That was my first time buying them clothes by myself. I had some good help by some great friends tho. I didn't get any hate mail or bad news from my wife.

My anxiety was manageable and so was my depression. Now all I'm looking forward to for the rest of the week is Wednesday night with the kids and then Friday night with some friends again. That's going to make the week drag but def looking forward to events during this week.

I just had to share some good news vs the normal bad news I normally post.

Part 3

Gathering Up My Shit

"…running Baby Daddy over with a car was not going to satiate her need for vengeance."

-Myself

Chapter 76

Sleeping Again after You Pee

I hated him the second he walked through the bar door. No, that's not entirely true. I'm pretty sure I hated him before he even got there. He was my twelfth date in four days. He was a reaction to the residual trauma that I had unearthed a week prior, after I finished being filmed for a documentary on John's suicide and widowhood. I had left the emotional security of San Diego and traveled back up to the small desert town John and I had spent our entire lives in, to be followed around by a camera for five days in a row, verbally and physically reliving every detail about his affairs and death.

The whole time I was being filmed, it felt like everything had happened yesterday, but it also felt like everything had happened a hundred years ago and to someone else. The shit-flavored icing on the shit-flavored cake that week was that I also put our former home up for sale while I was there and moved the last of our stuff out. Sobriety and celibacy were out of the question.

So yes, I knew before my date got there that I hated him. I could tell that he was unsure about his feelings for me as he pulled up the barstool to my left, so I made sure he shared my hatred by the end of the first drink. I was my most annoying, pessimistic self. Men in San Diego hate this. They all want their women to be thin, blond, and—above all else—optimistically Zen. They want us to have "good vibes" and shit. They want us to be passive, submissive, and stupid. They also want us to be vegan. Fuck all of this.

I am going to refer to my date as Prince Eric Jr., because I don't remember his real name, and because he was a redhead (doing a redhead had recently been added to my fuck-it list, not to be confused with a bucket list), and when I showed pictures to Amber later, she thought that he looked like Prince Eric and Ariel's love child.

As my date with Prince Eric Jr. dragged on into three-drink territory, it was evident that we both hated each other when I pointed out that his online dating picture was attractive and that he was not, and then he countered with a remark about how my profile failed to mention that I was a bitch. By drink four we were tied, insult to insult, eye roll to eye roll, glare for glare, but we both stood our ground like the pessimistic non-vegans that we were, daring the other one to wave the white flag and leave the date first. We stayed when the bartender announced that the kitchen would be closing soon, we stayed when that same bartender announced last call, we stayed when the last customer left, and we stayed a few more minutes after the manager asked us to leave.

I didn't know why at the time, but I offered to drive him home. He accepted. The car ride was silent. I couldn't bring myself to even turn on the radio. The atmosphere was oddly intimate. It was intimate, and it was hateful. It was like we were an old married couple leaving our fiftieth wedding-anniversary celebration and were exhausted from pretending that we had been happy for even one moment of our five decades together. It felt like we had a long history of hatred that had morphed into resentment and then settled into indifference somewhere around year thirty. It felt like a glimpse into the future I would've had with John's sick brain.

As we drove on, I could feel Prince Eric Jr.'s hatred of me and of all women everywhere rising, but it didn't feel uncomfortable or the least bit frightening. It felt comforting that he would openly and silently share his rage with me. It also felt honest and violating, like I was inside his head; I liked this violation, and I needed this honesty. As I drove on, I became aware that Prince Eric Jr.'s hatred didn't just live inside him, it lived inside the molecules of the air in the car, too—or was that my hatred? Somewhere along the midnight drive, the molecules of our mutual hatred became indistinguishable from each other as my car made its way through the zigzagging streets, directed only by Prince Eric Jr.'s index finger.

I stopped in front of his apartment building so abruptly that the momentum jolted us both forward. It was then that I realized neither of us had been wearing seatbelts. "Well, bye," I said, urging him to get out of my car. "I'd thank you for the drinks, but you didn't buy them, so…"

And then he kissed me. *He* kissed *me*. I did not kiss him back. I was irate at this aggressive gesture…I pushed him off me and began slapping him. He grabbed my wrists, pushed them down to my sides, and kissed me again. I did not kiss him back. He pulled away, looked straight into my eyes, and with one hand on my breast and one hand around my neck, he pinned me against the seat of my car and kissed me again. I did not kiss him back…until I did.

"Park the car," he commanded, so I did. Right there in the middle of a cul-de-sac, in a part of town I had never been in, at 2:42 a.m. on a hot July morning. It was a Wednesday. He turned the car key, took it out of the ignition, and placed it in the pocket of his jeans. He reached over to my right thigh. I wanted him to be impressed by the boldness I had to not be wearing panties under my unassuming white sundress on a first date as he put his right hand up my dress, but he wasn't. I could tell he expected no less from someone like me. It was when his left hand grasped my hair that I knew I could trust him. He proceeded to drag me from the car and lead me back to his apartment, using my hair as a leash. His other hand remained between my legs. All I could see were the stars.

I'm not going to go into the physical details of what happened in his loft. Even if I wanted to, I couldn't describe all the things that took place, and even if I could describe all the things that took place, I wouldn't, because this closing chapter isn't about the fucking. What I will tell you is that Prince Eric Jr. and I actively glared at each other and rarely broke eye contact. I will tell you that when the condom broke, he said to me with disgust, "That's your problem," and I slapped him harder than I've ever slapped a man.

I will tell you that I know what his blood tastes like, and he knows the flavor of mine, and I will tell you that when it was all over, the hatred that I had carried for my husband since his infidelities nearly six years ago had been forced out of me. Not only that, but I realized soon after this that the hatred I had for my husband was never fully for him; it had been mostly for myself. I didn't just hate the *fact* that I couldn't save John. I hated *who I was* because of my inability to love him back to salvation.

Prince Eric Jr. had taken this all from me, and he had thrown it away at the precise moment I forced myself to let it go. Somewhere in the midst of the slapping, biting, yelling, choking, and hair pulling, I hit my threshold for pain and unconsciously decided that enough was enough, that it wasn't my fault, and that it wasn't John's fault, either. I never climaxed, and Prince Eric Jr. and I never spoke again.

When I got home that morning, for the first time since the masturbation videos six years ago, I slept for ten hours straight. Then I woke up, peed, and slept for two more. Months later, I would have the epiphany that regaining the ability to sleep again after I peed was forgiveness.

Lynnette loves to tell the story about how she tried to run her son's father over with her car. She, at the age for sixteen, had just given birth to a son, only to return from the hospital to find his father at a public park with another woman. I use the term "woman" loosely, as everyone in this scenario was under the age of eighteen. As Baby Daddy and his new girlfriend fled the scene, a bystander whom Lynnette described to me as "homeless looking" approached her car and taught her something that forever changed her life. Homeless-Looking Guy taught her about forgiveness.

As legend goes, Homeless-Looking Guy said something deep and profound, along the lines of how running Baby Daddy over with a car was not going to satiate her need for vengeance. The only true vengeance in life was to be happy. Something clicked inside of hormonal, lactating sixteen-year-old Lynnette that day, and she decided that her grudge against Baby Daddy had manifested as hate, and hate had almost manifested itself into a vehicular manslaughter charge. She would never again give someone the satisfaction of her hatred. To hate someone meant that she still loved that person, and she would not love someone who impregnated her only to be at a park with another woman the very same week she had given birth to his child. After this, Lynnette never attempted vehicular manslaughter again because she was too busy searching for things that made her and her little boy happy. Forgiveness for Lynnette had been a choice and an act of rebellion, one of self-respect.

Forgiveness for me didn't feel like a conscious choice. It wasn't something I added to my life; it was something that had always been there underneath the hate. Forgiveness, to me, felt like being relaxed enough to sleep again after I peed. It felt like returning to myself, only to find myself to be a different person and being OK with this. Forgiveness didn't feel like the end of my anger, but it did feel like the end of my hate. Once I had experienced the full weight of the hatred I had for myself and for John, I was ready to get rid of it—and so I did, without even realizing I had, and forgiveness was what was left over.

I don't know why forgiveness had to be revealed to me during a violent sexual encounter, and I don't know why it had to be chosen by Lynnette after a conversation with Homeless-Looking Guy, but I do know that forgiveness, like love and hate, is not a one-size-fits-all sort of thing. The experiences of love, forgiveness, and hate are as unique as the humans that are living them. Once upon a time, I lived love, and then I lived hate, and then I lived forgiveness, and now I am back to the love.

He was a widower with sad eyes and broad shoulders. We made each other laugh, and we never attempted to heal the other's grief because we both understood that grief is not a thing to be fixed. Relax…I'm not going to tell you that falling in love with Widower saved me and that we lived happily ever after. Life after this kind of loss is not a fairy tale, but it does require some saving from a hero. Only there was no need for Widower to be my hero because I had already saved myself by being brave enough to really experience all parts of the grief.

I still save myself every single damn day, because my mourning for John will happen to me every single damn day. My widower knows this, so he stands beside me and I beside him, toasting each other for things that only widows find to be amazing, like drinking vodka in moderation, sending our children to school with shoes on their feet, listening to love songs without throwing something in anger, remembering to plug in the Crock-Pot after we turn it on, and the ability to sleep again after we pee.

Can't Get Enough of Me?

Follow me on Instagram @Mouthy_Michelle

Purchase widow themed clothing and merchandise items from the Mouthy_Michelle Collection on WidowDarkThirty.com

Read my blog, watch, and listen to my TV and podcast interviews on MouthyMichellesMusings.com